VOYAGE TO THE ICE

The Antarctic Expedition of
SOLO

VOYAGE TO THE ICE

The Antarctic Expedition of
SOLO

David Lewis

Published by the Australian Broadcasting Commission
in association with William Collins Sons & Co. Ltd
London, Glasgow, Sydney, Auckland, Toronto & Johannesburg

©1979 Australian Broadcasting Commission
145-153 Elizabeth Street, Sydney 2000
Postal Address: GPO 487, Sydney 2001

Australian Broadcasting Commission
National Library of Australia card number
and ISBN 0 642 97604 X

William Collins Sons & Co. Ltd
ISBN 0 00 216672 0

Printed and bound in Australia
by Griffin Press Limited

Typesetting by Photoset Computer Service Pty Ltd
Text type 10/11 Times Roman

Designed by Howard Binns-McDonald

Edited by Helen Findlay and Nina Riemer

Photographs supplied by Pieter Arriens, Peter Donaldson,
Jack Pittar, Ted Rayment and Dot Smith

Illustrations by Mike Gorman

CONTENTS

This book is dedicated to the crew of
Solo and to the organisers of the
expedition led by Yvonne Liechti and
Colin Putt.

'You may recall the sweep of savage splendour,
That land that measures each man at his worth
And feel in memory, half fierce, half tender,
The brotherhood of men that knew the South.'

**Douglas Mawson,
with apologies to Service**

**(Inscription in the copy of *Home of the Blizzard* that Mawson presented to
Edgeworth David, May 1915)**

Shadow of Disaster

The pale disc glowed briefly through a break in the mist, then disappeared again behind the overcast sky. The sun was low on the horizon for, despite the full daylight, it was two o'clock in the morning here hard by the Antarctic Circle. This one quick glimpse was enough to orientate ourselves; in the two hours since midnight the sun would have moved two hands' breadths or 30° to the left of south, so we had confirmation of our course. Such indications had become a necessity since, with the increasing proximity of the South Magnetic Pole, the steering compass had begun swinging wildly, pointing now north, now south, until it was useless.

The morning wore on; the wind was a very light northerly one and two swells had been running, one from the north-east and a second from the south-west. As the yacht sailed on southward the wind and the northerly swell remained the same but the swell from the south-west died away; the sea temperature dropped from −0.4°C to −0.9°. We peered ahead through the lightly falling snow searching for ice blink — the bright reflection in the sky that indicates the presence of ice-covered sea or land lying below — but the murk was too thick. Nevertheless, we knew that the damping down of the southerly swell coupled with the lowered sea temperature meant that the Polar pack must be close aboard.

The irregular white line barring the sea ahead came into view around half past eight that same morning. The date was January 3, 1978 and *Solo* was nineteen days out from Sydney, more than 1800 miles astern.

Our first objective, the bleak and storm-swept Antarctic Balleny Islands, lay no further than 100 miles south-east of our present position, but information, based on satellite photographs of the pack and received by radio, made it clear that a great tongue of ice intervened, ice which extended across our front 150 miles or more to the eastward, while everywhere in the west the main body of the pack constituted an impenetrable barrier. It would be necessary to work east along the margin, probing for gaps, until we could round the heavier concentrations of the drifting mass.

Conditions were ideal except for the ubiquitous mist and the snow showers. The fair breeze held and *Solo,* under number 2 jib, storm jib, trysail and mizzen, steadily closed the line of close-packed jumbled floes. They were jammed tightly together, we saw as we came nearer, and were often rafted one upon the other, their tilted weathered slabs mute witnesses to the enormous pressures to which they had been subjected. I recalled how Shackleton's *Endurance,* whose massive stem had been a full two metres thick, had been crushed like a matchbox by the Weddell Sea pack — and I shuddered; *Solo's* steel sides were only 5 mm thick. But outweighing this twinge of fear by far was excitement and a sense of coming home — back to the mystery and beauty of the polar sea.

Now we were but fifty metres off and it was time to alter course and turn east along the floating ice margin. The low grumble of floes grinding together added a new accompaniment to the accustomed hiss of the bow wave and creaking of the blocks — a background rumble that was soon to become so familiar as to be disregarded by the ear. Ever and anon the muttering rose to a crescendo as an ocean swell rolled booming into some purple cavern. More ominous, because silent and sinister, were the green underwater spurs that projected towards us to starboard, for these could rend a ship as readily as any rock.

The ice edge was serpiginous, often fronted by mile-long detached patches, and fringed with scattered outliers. Fields of very open pack alternated with close-set masses of floes. This way and that I spun the wheel and the yacht twisted and turned, apparently heading in a generally south-easterly direction according to the compass, which seemed to have steadied a little. Then around eleven the sun broke through again and revealed the humiliating fact that I had unwittingly turned the boat round so that she was pointing back northwards.

'Never in all my years in Greenland and the Antarctic have I worn so many clothes and yet felt so cold' remarked Lars Larsen, as he took over the helm and began stamping his feet on the steel deck. 'Working with the dogs, you have fed them and put up your tent and, within an hour of stopping, you are warm in your sleeping bag cooking supper — but this standing still at the wheel . . .' He wiped the snow from his face with a mittened hand.

The fog became denser, though paradoxically the glow of the sun could be discerned more often. Between times we steered by lining up the floes ahead. As we penetrated deeper into the loose pack what remained of the swell was damped until all that was left was a gentle undulation, for all the world as if the ice-clad ocean were breathing in quiet sleep. Our world was silent now; no living thing stirred, neither sea birds, nor penguins, seals, nor whales. The weathered and pressure-distorted silhouettes of the floes that loomed up and slid past in the shimmering fog took on an unreal dreamlike quality. Midnight came and went as we zig-zagged on through the silence.

Abruptly, somewhere around three o'clock in the morning of January 4, an impenetrable wall of jumbled floes reared up across our track. We turned back northward then, but not until six hours later were we in the clear, in open pack that covered no more than one eighth of the sea's surface. The course towards the east was resumed. To starboard ice blink reflected the heavy pack; the mist was clearing and the breeze freshening. *Solo* was moving a little more briskly, though still only at four to five knots.

The responsibility for the accident was mine. *Solo* carried a good deal more momentum than my familiar *Ice Bird* and it was a serious error of judgment on my part not to have reduced sail. Indeed, two of the crew, Lars Larsen and Pieter Arriens, called my attention to the fact that we were bumping the smaller floes with a good deal too much force. The warning came too late, however. Already the red bulkhead light indicating water in the bilge had come on and those on watch were anxiously hunting for the leak. We laboriously lifted out the heavy bags of provisions that filled the lazarette below the cockpit and under the after deck and piled them up, first in the cockpit until they overflowed, then along the side decks and all the way to the stern. Now that the storage space below was empty we could inspect it properly.

'No, it's not the propeller stern gland after all' called out Ted who was poking about. 'There's no sign of a leak here.'

This was the moment when Lars, searching beneath the floor boards of the forecabin, found it: a hole no larger than a finger's end, but through which a surprisingly large volume of sea water was spurting, had been punched through the starboard hull, three metres back from the stem and nearly a metre below the water line. It could only have been caused by impact with ice.

To plug the leak was the first essential. A cement patch was applied but kept lifting off with the water pressure until Fritz made a plug of neoprene, smeared it with butyl bostik from his wet suit repair kit, and forced it into the hole. Lars then mixed a fresh batch of cement, bagged it in Dot's pillow slip (how lucky we had a woman aboard who had brought anything so civilised, I thought), and tamped it down over Fritz's plug.

A rather tense half hour ensued before it became apparent that the cement was setting satisfactorily. An additional worry was the fear that there might be a general weakness in the whole plate — perhaps it had rusted paper thin and been missed at survey. This part of the hull *did* seem to bulge inwards rather ominously some thought, imagination beginning to run riot a little.

'We could bang it with a sledge hammer' suggested Lars, 'then we would know for sure how weak it is — but better, perhaps, that we wait till we get back to Sydney!'

'Hey, while you have that big bag of sugar out, pass me some for the galley, will you? And some freeze dried curry too. No, not the minced beef, the curry, and some green beans and milk.' Dot was taking the opportunity of the stores having been moved to restock the galley.

Here was one member of the crew at least whose morale had not been affected, I realised gratefully. But what about the others? How would this setback in our very first encounter with the Antarctic affect their willingness to continue? The leak itself had been repaired well enough and could easily be reinforced if necessary (in fact at the time of writing it has not yet been touched); I was not impressed by theories that surrounding steel plating, which had already stood up to three weeks' heavy pounding across the Southern Ocean, was ready to disintegrate. Clearly, *Solo's* ice capability had been somewhat reduced and we must proceed with greater caution.

For the time being everyone was working with a will, even if they were more subdued than usual. But the steps being taken were merely the obvious immediate ones to increase the seaworthiness of the ship:

jettisoning most of the heavy and bulky drums of emergency kerosene, for instance, so that we should have space to move aft the quantities of gear stowed in the forecabin and forepeak to raise the bow a little and to allow free access to the patch in case further work was required.

Meanwhile, Dot had dragooned Peter Donaldson into the role of quartermaster, and the two of them were systematically cataloguing the plastic bags of food as they were handed down and stowed below again. This essential procedure had been skimped during the loading at Sydney through sheer lack of time and manpower. For three hours this heavy work went on while *Solo* rocked gently without sail among the loosely scattered floes and brash ice and I took the opportunity to have a few quiet words with each individual, sounding them out and trying, very gently, to encourage positive thinking about the future of the expedition. Dot was obviously unshaken. Lars and Pieter Arriens were the most experienced in polar conditions and could be relied upon not to lose their sense of proportion and panic. But what of the rest?

Jack Pittar's sturdy common sense was as ever in evidence, I found. He would stand firm. Peter Donaldson, though understandably nervous, would go on. I sighed with relief. This quiet canvassing of attitudes had revealed a majority in favour of continuing with caution, but serious unexpressed fears could be sensed here and there. It was these that could yet wreck the expedition.

The situation was not one to be resolved by orders. We would hold a meeting before getting under way to decide future policy, I proposed, and everyone agreed. My sense of guilt at having misjudged the strength of the hull plating and so caused the accident in the first place weighed heavily upon my mind, but the same mistake would not be made again and I had no doubt whatsoever about the wisdom of continuing.

This was a case for very low key leadership; I must avoid any appearance of trying to pressure the meeting. But would the as yet unwelded and mostly inexperienced team come good in face of this early and harsh reminder of the menace lurking in the south? I was on tenterhooks and would be, not only until the meeting was over, even assuming a positive outcome, but for days or weeks until the crew's confidence in the ship and themselves should come back.

Our little company were certainly all on our own down here in 65° south. The Ballenys were only eighty-five miles from us now but separated from our position by impenetrable pack and, in any case, they offered no haven. The nearest port in New Zealand, Bluff, lay 1100 miles to the northward; Hobart 1320.

I recalled the origins of the enterprise, the plans, disappointments, the heart-breaking search for funds and the triumph and high hopes at our departure. Were these high hopes and the sacrifices of so many people to come to nothing? Were we going to fail their trust? I would soon know.

Chapter 1

Antarctica, the Last Frontier

I t had all begun in a blizzard in the Snowy Mountains in the winter of
1975. Or rather, a group of like minded people had happened to come
together then, as the wind howled and the tents shuddered under the
blast of the driving snow, and talk about the need for research expeditioners
to take up the cudgels for the marine world and its further shores. There
were Colin Putt and Ian Dillon, both with vast polar experience, Dot Smith,
Margaret Huenerbein, Patricia Pedersen, Grant Hawley and myself; all
people who were to form the nucleus of the future Oceanic Research
Foundation and who remain among its leadership today.

I remembered us squatting round the hissing primus stove and later
cradling steaming mugs of tea gratefully in our mittened hands, and how
the conversation came to centre on Antarctica — not unnaturally, perhaps,
in those surroundings.

'It is the size of Europe, and a lot nearer to us here than Perth is'
remarked Colin Putt who has an encyclopaedic memory. 'Australia claims
nearly half of it — forty per cent' he went on, 'yet we can't be spending more
than a couple of million a year, if that, and the Russians have twice as many
scientists in our sector as we have. What chance has this country to have
any real say in the future unless we — not just the government, I mean — do
a whole lot more to justify a claim like that?'

'What we need' I put in thoughtfully, 'is a group who can learn more
about Antarctic living. They can find out if there is a place for simple
technologies that save energy. I am sure there is. I mean things like the use
of sail and wind generators.'

Colin followed on quickly: 'We could easily fit a 30 metre trawler with
enough sail for the Southern Ocean passages. There is no lack of wind down
there. We could do a lot of useful researching on a very low budget. What
does it cost to run one of the Dan ships the government charters? Three or
four thousand a day, I wouldn't be surprised. Our whole summer
expedition could be run for less than their expenses for a week.'

'How much would a converted trawler cost, though?' Ian brought the
discussion sharply back to earth.

'It was hard enough raising the money to charter *Patanella* for Heard Island' Colin agreed. He had been a member of a remarkable private Antarctic expedition in 1964-65. Led by Warwick Deacock, with the veteran polar seaman and mountain explorer Bill Tilman as skipper, the party had not only sailed the 20 metre Tasmanian fishing schooner *Patanella* to storm-swept sub-Antarctic Heard Island, but had made the first ascent of its glacier-clad 3000 metre peak, Big Ben. That had been individual initiative with a vengeance. They had set a great example. Could it be followed up?

My own single-handed voyage to Antarctica in the 10 metre yacht *Ice Bird* in the 1972-73 and 1973-74 seasons had been first and foremost an adventure in which I had become the first lone sailor to breach the formidable defences of the frozen continent. This ultimate challenge of the sea had been met successfully, at the cost of terrors and hardships that I still could not bear to dwell upon. The experience had so sapped my courage that I had no stomach for another single-handed voyage, but it had paradoxically left me with a more profound involvement than ever with the terrible white South.

It was not adventure that drew me now, but a more mature commitment to learn some of the secrets of Antarctica; to play a part in bringing this last great frontier of the wilderness closer to the orbit of mankind while, at the same time, helping to protect it against destructive forms of exploitation. Very little thought was needed to make clear that lack of funds, the problem that Ian Dillon now brought up, was likely to prove the stumbling block to putting any such ambition into practice.

The obvious solution would be to join a government research organisation, like the Australian National Antarctic Research Expeditions (ANARE), for private individuals, however keen, could do no more than supplement the work of such agencies. On the other hand, ANARE had nailed its colours firmly to the mast of elaborate high-energy technology — tractor trains, helicopters and the like. Did this leave niches that could usefully be filled by more lightly equipped enthusiasts, I asked myself. The answer was a resounding 'yes'. Modern bases, big as they were, were but specks on the vast face of Antarctica. There remained ample scope for the man-hauled sledge-kyak and a hundred other low-energy ways of living and travelling. Pioneering groups would be ineffectual, however, unless they could speak with the voice of experience; in the case of Antarctica, experience meant expeditions. I was back where I had started from. Apart from becoming a cog in an existing machine, there was nothing for it but to set up an organisation from scratch. The practical problems were daunting but I resolved to try. This was even before that fortuitous encounter in the Snowy Mountains which proved to be the first breakthrough.

Where rests Antarctica's fascination? As a continent it is unique. This is not so much because it remains locked in the ice age for, after all, so are most of Greenland and the Arctic islands off Canada and Siberia. Remoteness is what renders the Antarctic so different from all other continents. This remoteness is such that it was not until the twenties of last century that man ever set foot upon its shores.

Nor was the first sighting so very much earlier. The Russian explorer Thadeus von Bellingshausen has the distinction of being the first man to see

Antarctica, though he supposed at the time that the snow-covered hills he saw were merely huge hummocks of ice. But it was land right enough, the Antarctic mainland in the region now known as Princess Martha Coast. This historic event took place on January 29, 1820.

Two days later and a thousand miles to the westward the British naval captain John Bransfield, having crossed the strait that now bears his name, became the second man to sight the long-hidden continent. His midshipman cannot have been much taken with the mountains of the Antarctic Peninsula that towered above the southern horizon, for he described the prospect as 'the most gloomy that can be imagined'.

The identity of the man who first set foot on Antarctica is less certain, the most likely contender for the honour being the New England sealing skipper John Davis, who landed briefly on the coast of the Antarctic Peninsula on February 7, 1821. The log entry recording this milestone is laconic in the extreme:

'10 A.M. Close in with it, out boat and send her on shore to look for seal.'

These were the first contacts with the new land, but they were fleeting ones. Not until the very close of the nineteenth century, 1899-1900 in point of fact, did a party actually winter over on the continent. This was at Cape Adare and the leader of the expedition was a young Norwegian-Australian named Carsten Borchgrevink. Both the place and the man come into our story later.

If we wonder why the great southern land remained virgin for so very long after the rest of the world had been peopled (even Greenland had been occupied for millennia by hardy Eskimos), the answer lies in the dread wastes of the Southern Ocean that completely girdle Antarctica. These are the stormiest waters on earth and thirty per cent of the part of the ocean that lies south of the 40th parallel has its surface frozen into restless grinding ice floes — the polar pack. Distances across the Southern Ocean to inhabited lands are immense. Towards Australia, for instance, the waste of wild water stretches for 1500 miles and matches the width of the North Atlantic. Only between Cape Horn and the Antarctic Peninsula, with its off-lying South Shetland Islands, does the expanse narrow to 500 miles or so. But Drake's Passage which, with Bransfield Strait, separates the two continents, is stormy even by Southern Ocean standards.

The Eskimos were able to reach Greenland over the narrow seas from the Canadian Arctic islands in their skin-covered *umiaks* and *kyaks*. Long ages later tenth century Norsemen from Iceland rowed their galleys up the Greenland fjords. But the wild waters of Drake's Passage below the Horn effectively barred the way to the beech bark canoes of the Alacalufe Indians of Tierra del Fuego. Nor were the twenty metre double canoes of those Pacific Vikings, the Polynesians, capable of venturing very far south of New Zealand. Legends to the contrary, scantily clad men in semi-open boats, even seamen of the calibre of the Maoris, could never have survived in the far south. As to the legends, these were recorded very late, when Maoris were already serving on European whaling ships in Antarctic waters.

So although parts of Antarctica are no more inhospitable than East Greenland where men have lived for untold ages, its shores remained unpeopled, unvisited and unknown. The discovery of Antarctica, when at last it came about, was the crowning achievement of the long age of sail.

Once the last frontier had been breached daring and ruthless men were soon on hand to exploit the discovery. The beautiful and intelligent fur seals were all but exterminated within the unbelievably short time of two decades. Even today, a century and a half later, remnants of once teeming colonies are only just beginning to re-establish themselves. After the fur seals had been killed for their skins it was the elephant seals' turn to be boiled down for their blubber. On Macquarie Island and elsewhere penguins joined them, and were herded *en masse* into the trying vats.

Nevertheless, some of the sealing captains, notably those employed by the British firm of Enderby Brothers, actively pushed back the frontier as explorers in their own right. Of this calibre were James Weddell, John Biscoe and John Balleny. The Americans John Davis and Nathaniel Palmer, master of the gallant little cutter, *Hero,* deserve to be included in their number. These were brave and extraordinarily hardy men, to whom all who came after owe a very great debt. But the trade they were engaged in typified the worst excesses of commercial greed. It was self-destructive for, when the breeding stocks of the seals had been liquidated, the industry itself abruptly vanished.

We are in no position to be smug about our Victorian forebears, however, seeing that a proposal for boiling down penguins for their fat is now being seriously considered. Then again, the short-sightedness of last century's sealers is fully matched by the contemporary whaling industry. In the days of the hand harpoon and the sailing ship, whaling was somewhat redeemed by the high courage of the hunters. An idea of the perils they faced can be gathered from the fact that in 1830, no less than twenty whaling ships were crushed by the Arctic ice in Melville Bay alone. Today the 'take' of whales is subject to international agreements, though these are less effective, one feels, than the growing scarcity of whales.

We have good cause, then, to ponder on the destiny of Antarctica and the stormy ocean that surrounds it. The southern waters teem with krill, the tiny shrimp-like crustacean upon which the huge blue whales were wont to feed. There are rich fishing grounds too. Already trawlers from West Germany, Poland, the Soviet Union and Japan have begun large-scale harvesting of krill and more conventional fishing besides.

In themselves these developments are not necessarily bad. More people and depleted world resources must of necessity bring increased human activity to the less accessible parts of the globe, Antarctica among them. Krill has been estimated by the Australian Minister for Science to be capable of more than doubling the sea's yield of edible protein. But in default of more knowledge about breeding cycles, distribution and regenerative capacity, it could easily be fished out. In that event, not only would human beings be the losers but also seals, penguins, whales and seabirds that all depend upon krill for a large part of their sustenance. Many more studies are needed.

What has been said about marine resources applies with equal force, if a little further in the future, to oil and minerals. The prospects for these are

Facing page • *top* **David Lewis** *bottom* **Lars Larsen**
Following pages • *top* **Peter Donaldson** *bottom* **Dot Smith**
top **Jack Pittar** *bottom* **Ted Rayment**

bound to grow steadily more attractive as they become exhausted elsewhere. Current studies on the likely effects of development on the Antarctic environment are inadequate and there is doubt whether those proposed will be uninfluenced by political and economic pressures.

Though Antarctica presents a facade of unalterable stability, it is in reality extremely vulnerable to human intervention. Take smog, for instance. Ninety per cent of the earth's fresh water is locked up in the Antarctic ice cap. The advent of any appreciable smog would greatly speed the rate of melting; the resulting floods would be incalculable. Another example is that the breakdown of waste matter by bacterial action, that we take for granted elsewhere, is virtually absent in Antarctica, where the temperatures generally remain below freezing all the year round. Yet an Argentine Antarctic settlement is already in being (the first child has been born there); it must be only a matter of time before hotel complexes, mining camps, oil rigs, ports and airfields make their appearance.

Technology is certainly capable of solving the considerable problems involved. It is *how* they are tackled that matters. We can either live *with* the Antarctic by studying its ecology and adjusting our activities to fit in, or we can forcibly overcome and so disrupt the delicate balances. At one extreme is the option of throwing the white wilderness open to uncontrolled development, no doubt under the nominal umbrella of international agreement. The opposite view is that the continent should be kept in 'cold storage' (no pun intended) as a mammoth laboratory. This may be desirable but impracticable in view of political and economic realities.

A third and, to my mind, more suitable option would be to declare the whole continent a kind of 'International Park', or a series of national parks run by separate countries. This would demand immediate ecological research to provide guide lines as to what developments could be safely undertaken — the types of tourism and the locations, for instance. Comprehensive studies of this sort would save many later mistakes that would be costly in terms both of environmental and wildlife destruction and wasted money and effort.

A start of a sort has already been made, for it was just such considerations that led to the signing of the Antarctic Treaty in 1959. Nineteen nations are now parties to it. Seven (Argentina, Australia, Britain, Chile, France, New Zealand and Norway) have territorial claims, though these are not recognised by the two whose Antarctic effort is greatest, the United States and the Soviet Union, and it has been agreed that claims to sovereignty shall be held in abeyance for the duration of the treaty. As it stands, the treaty provides for the exchange of scientific information and lays down rules for the protection of the continental environment. But it does not cover the offshore pack, and it is here that sealing and penguin culling are likely to be resumed and oil drilling instituted.* Nor is there any consensus as to what will happen when the treaty expires in 1990.

---

* A Seal Convention has now been ratified, allowing annual quotas of 175 000 Crabeaters, 12 000 Leopards and 5000 Weddells. Elephant, Ross and fur seals are totally protected.

Facing page • *top* **Pieter Arriens** *bottom* **Fritz Schaumberg**

It must be obvious that our embryo group of would-be unofficial researchers was proposing to move into waters politically as stormy as those of the Southern Ocean. It took an effort of will, in a field so dominated by the big batallions, to hold to the belief that independents, operating on a small budget to conduct low-key research, had any part to play.

Chapter 2

The Enterprise takes Shape

The task of setting up any sort of informal association capable of mounting the smallest Antarctic expedition seemed beyond the scope of a few obscure individuals. After all, we had neither a vessel nor funds to buy or charter one. Common sense dictated that we give up such an impractical dream. What gave us the courage to go ahead was the example of the pioneer explorers. They had never acknowledged any common sense limits either and had gone on to accomplish the impossible.

Take Borchgrevink, for example. He was without money or influence. The Royal Geographical Society, intent on backing only such acceptable explorers as naval officers, would have none of him. Nothing daunted, the determined young man paid his own fare from Australia to London, where he so impressed the newspaper proprietor Sir George Newnes, that the press magnate agreed to finance his expedition of 1899-1900.

Not only the unknown Borchgrevink, but other pioneers whose names are household words, had to scheme and struggle and use every means to finance their venture. Thus Shackleton was not too proud to beg for support and, on one occasion, he dressed three men in polar costume and had them parade through the streets of London advertising a fund-raising meeting. Things were not laid on for Mawson or Wilkins either. Every one of these great explorers had had to go cap in hand to wealthy individuals and government departments. They all met slights and disappointments that would have deterred any ordinary mortal. But they never gave in.

There was much to be said, the positive Colin Putt remarked, for participants organising their own expeditions. Their informality allowed them to be more economical, practical and flexible in their planning than the more massive institutions. The latter were, of course, necessary for national programs. But Colin's experience of the private *Patanella* expedition to Heard Island and his and Ian Dillon's participation in one of Tilman's equally informal expeditions to Greenland in the cutter *Sea Breeze* had taught them that there was another and simpler way, one that paid off in efficiency and results. If only the finance hurdle could be surmounted.

Shackleton's fund-raising group in London

Our first idea of what was eventually to become the Oceanic Research Foundation was an association of researcher-expeditioners who would each contribute a share towards the purchase of a vessel and other expenses. We optimistically started a society of this sort and proposed to pool our resources and bring in more shareholders. Each participant would put in $2000, become a joint owner of the ship and be entitled to take part in expeditions. But the cheapest suitable second-hand vessel was found to cost in the region of $120 000. A little calculation showed that sixty shares would be needed to buy the boat and something like fifteen more to launch an expedition — seventy-five people entitled to participate. Since the boat could carry no more than fifteen at any one time, the shareholders would have to wait five years for their turn. Thus, this particular company of Antarctica was stillborn.

At this jucture a captain of industry, who had been impressed with my researches into Polynesian navigation, unexpectedly came to our aid. He advised an entirely new tack — the setting up of a non-profit research foundation that could appeal to the public for funds. It was essential, in his view, that we seek tax deductible status for donations. He himself would provide the services of lawyers and accountants and engage a professional fund raising firm for a feasibility study. He was as good as his word.

A permanent addition to our forces now arrived from Canada in the person of Yvonne Liechti. She had been the Canadian correspondent whom I mentioned in my book *Ice Bird* as having been disillusioned when she saw in a *National Geographic* picture what a disreputable-looking old sea dog I really was. Nevertheless, the next time I went to Washington she flew down from Canada to meet me. She subsequently twice visited Australia. Yvonne is a businesswoman with public relations experience; equally important, she loves the outdoors and the sea, though the winters in Montreal have effectively cured her of any liking for cold climates. She was later to become secretary-treasurer of the foundation, after her vigilance had steered it away from a near disaster — as we shall see later. She is now my wife.

It would be tedious to go through all the study documents that we and the fund raisers prepared or to detail the discussions with the taxation authorities, the Commonwealth Scientific and Industrial Research Organisation (CSIRO) and other bodies. Innumerable letters were written to potential supporters. Months dragged by while the fund raisers deliberated. Ultimately there emerged from their labours a plan for a million dollar foundation, top heavy with sub-committees, a bureaucracy more monstrous by far than any civil servant's nightmare. The project was viable, they said. Maybe it was, but not for us. Our intention had been and remained to set up a lean and spare organisation of enthusiasts with just as much top hamper as was needed to get the job done.

The captain of industry was not pleased either. Not unreasonably he rejected the fund raiser's proposal, which would have cost him more than a little. Regrettably, he went further and washed his hands of the incipient foundation altogether, on the not altogether unreasonable grounds that I lacked the charisma of leadership and dynamic forcefulness, and so was unlikely to win the support of hard-headed business men. (I am, in fact, a low key person.)

This was a heavy blow. We were now well into 1977, the year of our proposed first expedition, and the ground was suddenly taken from under our feet. Without the continued confidence of Colin and Yvonne the blow would have been mortal. We had the rudiments of our foundation, they pointed out; we had learned many important lessons in the unfamiliar field of fund raising; we must press on. We did.

A most helpful relationship with a firm that travelled in the same direction as us for a time marked the next stage, and this took us a long way towards clarifying our aims and presenting our first brochure. A number of prominent people in Australia and abroad had already agreed to become foundation members; our presentation was well received.

Dr Pieter Arriens, a geophysicist who had returned from a year as officer-in-charge of the Australian Antarctic base at Davis (not his only southern experience by any means), now began to play a valuable part. He was instrumental in setting up a strong scientific committee and his contacts with the scientific community in general and Antarctic scientists in particular greatly facilitated the planning of the forthcoming expedition. I had first met Pieter several years before during an igloo-building excursion in the Snowy Mountains. He, in turn, introduced Lars Larsen, a Dane who had spent the previous year as radio operator at Mawson Antarctic base. The versatile Lars had for two years been a member of the North Greenland sledge dog patrol and was a graduate of the famous Norwegian Army Arctic School, as well as being an experienced seaman. He was to become the executive officer and deputy leader aboard *Solo*.

A good deal of travelling now became the order of the day: to Canberra again to meet the very helpful Senator Webster, the Minister for Science, and the first Australian minister responsible for Antarctic affairs to personally visit the land in his charge. Then to Melbourne, where the Antarctic and Meteorological divisions of the Department of Science had their headquarters, and which became the focus of activity for Pieter Arriens and myself. Facilities for radio communication, help in planning the scientific program and advice on logistics were forthcoming in full measure, the ANARE scientists and field personnel being particularly helpful. Of course there was no question of government funds being channelled our way (short of undertaking some contract assignment — a matter hopefully for the future). Nor, although we were woefully short of money, did we ask for any from that source, for to have accepted government funding would inevitably have meant the loss of our precious independence. Instead, we concentrated on drafting appeals to industry and commerce, appeals which in the main met with a disappointing response.

Despite uncertainties aplenty, all seemed set fair for an expedition in the summer of 1977-78. It was Yvonne who recognised the true significance of one small dark cloud on the horizon.

The firm whose collaboration with us was proving so fruitful held an option on a sturdy and roomy motor-sailer, a suitable vessel for our needs. This they proposed to charter to us and things had gone so far that Lars Larsen was actually living aboard in the capacity of unpaid engineer to learn the workings of the ship. The rub was this. The Oceanic Research Foundation (ORF) was a non-profit organisation. Yet two members of the commercial firm were on our provisional board of directors, one being our managing director; we were using their lawyers, accountants and premises. There was nothing inherently wrong with this arrangement, except that chartering the firm's boat at terms set by themselves alone could be open to abuse. It would leave a loophole through which donations to the foundation might conceivably be siphoned off. Matters came to a head when the firm's representatives took offence at Yvonne's daring to ask perfectly legitimate questions about charter fees and an option to purchase the vessel. Something had to change — but what? I was prepared to resign if the Foundation could be saved that way. The boat, so tantalisingly dangled before us, had both Colin and me hypnotised a little. Its importance loomed very large indeed and there could be no gainsaying that in default of a vessel there could be no expedition — and no other ship was on the horizon.

It was the dynamic Dick Smith who now came on the stage. Dick is a bundle of energy, a young man far too positive and many-sided to be readily summed up. A brilliant electronics engineer and businessman, he enlivened his early apprenticeship with daring climbs up the dizzy arches of Sydney's harbour bridge, to the despair of the police who never managed to catch him. Not surprisingly, Dick became a skilled rock climber. One of his mentors, Colin Putt, was impressed with his character. 'I will never forget his keenness,' he recalled. Dick's interests turned to flying, when he conceived the ambition of piloting his own plane to Antarctica. Baulked in this for the time being, he organised flights in 747s for tourists across the polar circle. On one of these flights we met.

Our liking was immediate and mutual and from that moment on Dick took an active part in the Foundation. Later he became our first Fellow (Grant Hawley, our Torres Strait researcher and veteran of the Snowy Mountains weekend, was the second) and Lord Shackleton, son of the

22

famous explorer, became our patron. Neither Colin nor I are businessmen; now at last Yvonne had someone of her own calibre to turn to. The existing mélange of non-profit and commercial companies could lead only to disaster, Dick confirmed. No sensible donor would dream of investing in an enterprise where such patent possibilities for misappropriation existed, and he doubted very much whether the tax authorities would wear it either. The ORF must not only be financially above reproach, it must be seen to be so.

The upshot was that I issued an ultimatum to our friends insisting on the complete separation of the two entities: the firm's two directors must resign from the Foundation; any contractual relationships, including charter agreements, must be arranged through each party's own solicitors. The firm had no option but to accept.

Our board was strengthened by the addition of Margaret Huenerbein, another of the original Snowy Mountains party. Unfortunately she was committed to a Himalayan trek otherwise she would have been a member of the expedition as well. It was now June. We bent all our efforts towards the official launching of the foundation, though I had to take time off to do a month-long locum in general practice simply to keep the wolf from the door. Dick Smith continued to be a tower of strength. At this stage we still believed that the promised vessel would be chartered to us. Only as month followed month did the evasiveness of our erstwhile colleagues and their refusal to discuss concrete terms force us to the unwelcome conclusion that a ship must be sought elsewhere.

This was a pretty kettle of fish — an expedition like to be stillborn for lack of transport; a monumental anticlimax. The timing of polar voyages is strictly controlled by the date of the break-up of the consolidated winter pack; mid-December was our deadline and spring was fast approaching. On a more personal plane my morale was in no wise helped by the imminence of my sixtieth birthday, 'Daddy's D Day,' as my daughters irreverently called it, a reminder of the passage of time that I could well have done without. The foundation was to be launched in mid-September, though official approval of our tax deductible status would not be forthcoming until the following year. The search for a boat was renewed, but not a single strong work boat was available at a price we could afford.

An advertisement in a newspaper momentarily caught my eye. I checked, shrugged and read on. Then I turned back a page and re-read the advertisement with care. The idea seemed crazy, but was it? A moment later I was telephoning Colin.

'A racing yacht!' His tone showed his scepticism.

'Yes, I have had enough of yachts in the Antarctic. But this is *Solo!*'

'Oh, *Solo.*' The tone changed. 'She has twice won the Sydney-Hobart hasn't she? And she has been round the world. Didn't she pile up once in Magellan Strait? She must be strong and a damn good seaboat.'

'*Solo* is narrow and must be very short of storage space,' I put in. 'Could she possibly carry about eight people and the couple of tons of stores that we would need? They say she is a bit of a submarine at the best of times.' I was beginning to regret having even contemplated the yacht.

'Only one way to find out,' replied Colin cheerfully. 'Let's go down and look her over.'

We found *Solo* at a marina in Rushcutters Bay. My heart sank as I studied her ultra slender lines and noted how low in the water she lay even when unladen. Her freeboard was no greater than that of my own 9.7 metre *Ice Bird,* a yacht less than a third *Solo's* size (displacement). Only at the bow did the raised bulwarks, the 'cow catcher,' offer some prospect of protection for the crew. I glanced down at the sheet of statistics the broker had supplied: length 17.4 metres, breadth 4.4 metres, draft 2.4 metres — she was deep enough anyway, drawing a full eight feet unloaded. The tall main mast towered 19.5 metres above the deck (it was later to cause us some anxiety when passing beneath the sagging power lines to Dangar Island). The steel hull plating, I read, was 4.75 mm thick, the deck 3.2 mm — not overly stout for ice in view of the momentum that the yacht's thirty-five odd tons would impart. The fuel and water tanks were copious, I saw with satisfaction — 1824 litres of diesel fuel and 912 litres of fresh water.

Colin and I clambered aboard. The layout was well planned and the equipment well maintained, evidence of the seamanship and engineering ability of the owner, the noted Vic Meyers. The 100 hp diesel engine was centrally placed beneath the saloon table, easily accessible. A clutch and generator were fitted to the shaft so that the batteries could be charged by the free-wheeling propellor under sail without need to run the main engine or the auxiliary generator, a boon on a long-distance sailing yacht, where charging batteries without wasting fuel is always a problem. The cabin insulation was more than adequate, being a good nine cm thick on the average. The instrumentation was also excellent. It included a radar, I noted gratefully, recalling with a shudder the many near misses when I was on my own in 1974 and bergs had materialised out of the mist and driving snow ahead with uncanny abruptness. Yes, it would be good to have radar (I was not to know then that cold and damp would render it inoperative until the closing stages of our voyage). There was an autopilot, which promised to be a boon until its in-built compass should fail towards the South Magnetic Pole; a log that registered both speed and distance; a wind speed indicator (inoperative); an old radio transmitter that Vic Meyers remarked later could reach Double Bay in 'good conditions' (a couple of miles). Fortunately, Maurice Findlay was to supply us with a pair of excellent 'Stingray' sets in its place. Likewise the ancient chronometer; Phillips were to make good that deficiency with a quartz crystal instrument.

'More stowage room down here than I thought' Colin called approvingly, emerging from the lazarette beneath the cockpit and after cabin. 'No need down south for those light weather sails that take up so much room.'

'I don't see how we can make more than five or six of the bunks usable at sea' I worried. 'Those two just inside the cabin would have to be left free for people on watch to sit in shelter.' This was a very serious disadvantage. We envisaged a minimum crew of eight, so that four could be put ashore at any one time leaving four to look after the ship. There would be no huts or harbours and sea ice and weather conditions could change in a flash, so that both parties must be strong and self-sufficient. The necessity to 'hot bunk' would deprive us of those little private corners where one's own belongings could be stowed undisturbed. Everyone needs his own personal living space where he can 'switch off' and be alone and private for a while. This near-necessity, a bunk apiece, would not be practicable on *Solo*.

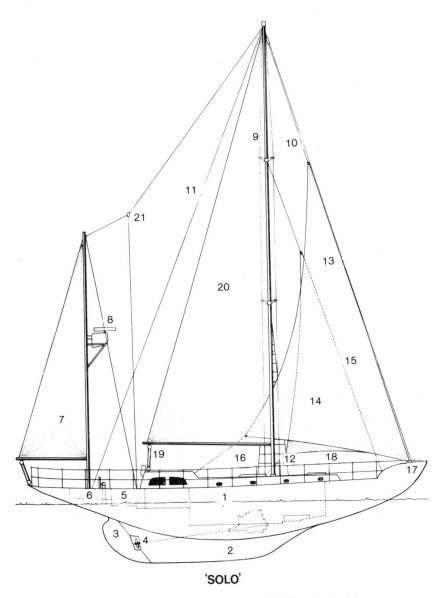

'SOLO'

1 Hull	12 Ratlines (port only)
2 Keel	supporting mast
3 Rudder	13 No.2 or No.1 jib
4 Propeller	14 No.3 or storm jib
5 Cockpit with wheel, compass binnacle	15 Inner forestay
and auto-pilot	16 Jib sheets
6 Sheeting well with winch	17 'Cow catcher'
7 Mizzen mast, sail and boom	18 Rails and stanchions
8 Radar	19 Main sheet and sheet winch
9 Main mast	20 Main sail
10 Twin forestays	21 Radio antenna
11 Stays (shrouds)	
supporting mast	

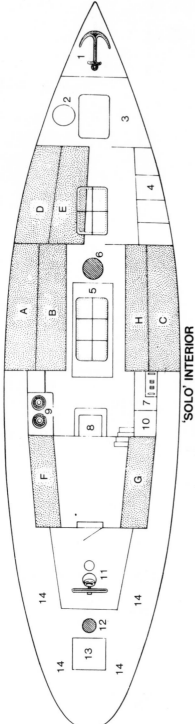

'SOLO' INTERIOR

1 Anchor stowage
2 Toilet (skylight over)
3 Sail, ski and ice axe stowage
4 ABC camera equipment stowage
5 Table, engine under, (skylight over)
6 Main mast
7 Radios and oilskin stowage
8 Galley sink (blocked off)
9 Galley
10 Chart table
11 Cockpit with wheel, binnacle (compass) & auto-pilot
12 Mizzen mast
13 Sheeting well
14 Lazarette under part of cabin & cockpit
A, B, C, D & E Permanent bunks
F, G, & H Seats sometimes used as bunks

To make matters worse, the yacht's large cabins were open plan, so that all activities — cooking, radio operation, writing up scientific log books, navigation, eating, sleeping and the rest must be conducted in two interconnected rooms. It was not hard to imagine the congestion, when every locker would be crammed with food, clothing, tools, instruments, reference books and equipment and the very floor piled high with kitbags, sacks of vegetables and polar boots. The expedition, if we chose *Solo,* was bound to be an extraordinarily uncomfortable one. Could any crew be expected to tolerate such overcrowding in arctic conditions for something like three months?

Meanwhile Colin had been measuring and calculating.

'*Solo* will go down in the water by the best part of a third of a metre when she is fully loaded' he announced. 'That will not be so bad if she is not driven hard. Extra cans of water, the outboards, life raft and inflatables can all be lashed on deck without impairing stability at all.'

'A canvas dodger right round the deck along the rails, continuing the line of the cow catcher, would make life a good deal more bearable for the crew' I added.

Very thoughtful were the two of us as we drove home that night. In *Solo's* favour was the fact that she was a proven seaboat; she could be expected to stand up to anything the Southern Ocean might throw at her. Then there was her legendary performance, the very thought of which was enough to make any sailor's pulse beat faster. Against, were the limited accommodation and storage space. Moreover the yacht's price was $60 000. How we were to raise this remained to be seen.

This first inspection of *Solo* took place at the end of August, but a final decision about her had to await the results of the Foundation's inaugural and fund raising meeting on September 17. This meeting was sponsored by Dick Smith. He hired the hall, circularised his airborne expeditioners and donated a ticket on his next Antarctic flight as a raffle prize. Additional prizes were superb air shots of Antarctica that photographer Jutta Malnic gave us. The famous Frank Hurley film was shown of Shackleton's *Endurance* being crushed by the ice — not an omen for us, I hoped. Willing helpers, too numerous to mention, sold T-shirts, books and raffle tickets. Altogether the evening was a huge success. Nearly $2 000 was raised apart from the *pièce de résistance,* a donation of $10 000 from Dick. This was a particularly generous gesture since there was no guarantee at this stage that tax deductibility would ever be granted.

At least we were solvent. Several smaller sums, together with my own $4000 and the faithful Grant Hawley's $1000, were already in the kitty. Later Margaret Huenerbein added $2000 that she could ill afford and donations came in from New Zealand and the USA as well as Australia. All this was more than encouraging but we were still far short of the $60 000 we needed. Nevertheless, we decided to take the plunge and on October 4 put down $6000 deposit on the yacht.

Our lawyer was appalled. There was no guarantee of our being able to fulfil our obligations, he pointed out. Various grants we had applied for had already been turned down; what certainty did we have that we could raise the balance in time? This was crushing. We were not certain at all. Overwhelmed by the enormity of what we had done, above all at the responsibility we bore for other people's money, Yvonne and I never once slept soundly for a fortnight. Meanwhile the bank, not without a good deal of prodding from Yvonne, agreed to lend us $30 000 provided we could find adequate security. Yvonne and I had little left to offer by this time but Fritz Schaumberg, the Putts and Margaret Huenerbein stepped into the breach by mortgaging their homes.

I make no apology for going into such detail about our financial struggles, for they were no less decisive battles than any that followed with the ice and the Southern Ocean and they laid the basis for the whole undertaking. Nor would it be fair to gloss over the efforts of the hundreds of anonymous donors and helpers who made success possible. I want also to counter a common misconception. People sometimes remark how 'lucky' we are to have time to run expeditions, the clear implication being that the speaker, by contrast, is far too busy with serious concerns for such frivolity. Busy indeed! I am sure that Yvonne, Colin and I have never worked so hard or worried so much as we did, and are still doing, over the Foundation.

Once the bank loan had been secured there still remained the balance of the $30 000 we must raise ourselves — a matter of $5000 only, but still a sum beyond our immediate reach. Try as we would this yawning gap remained until the Australian Broadcasting Commission waved its magic wand and came up with contracts for a television film and a book about the voyage.* The Foundation became the owners of *Solo* on October 31, 1977.

Four days later, somewhat overawed by the length of ship I had to manoeuvre between the close-moored yachts, I took the helm. With glad hearts and a fair wind we swept out to sea and up the coast fifteen miles to Barrenjoey Head, where we hauled our wind for the Hawkesbury Estuary. It was seven miles up the winding mile-wide river to our headquarters at Dangar Island; the breeze died away and we had to motor. On either hand the bush-clad sandstone bluffs rose ever higher, while the equally forested island gradually detached itself from its background. Most of the houses of its 150 inhabitants (including our own) were effectively screened from view by the trees. As we moored in their shadow, rainbow lorikeets flashed by in streaks of brilliant colour and pink hibiscus blossoms overhung the warm muddy water. An unlikely locale, I thought, in which to prepare an Antarctic expedition.

Time was not on our side. Satellite ice reports interpreted by the glaciologist, Dr Bill Budd, from Melbourne University, suggested that the Balleny Islands-Cape Adare region might be accessible early in the season and that a start by mid-December was indicated. So December 15 it was to be, little enough time in all conscience to carry out a major refit and put together a full scale expedition, for this scheduled date of departure was now no more than a month and a half away. If this seemed an impossibly short time, we remembered how the setting up of the Foundation in the first place had appeared just as impractical. There was nothing for it but to set to work with a will.

The members of the crew had in the main been selected by this time and I am often asked how they were chosen. In the first place there were certain

---

* *VOYAGE TO THE ICE,* ABC television special, first screened throughout Australia Sept 27, 1978.

28

essential trades and skills that must be covered. These included seamanship and navigation, ice pilotage, diesel mechanics, radio operation, biology, geology, meteorology and mountaineering (landing in the Antarctic is equivalent to stepping ashore onto New Zealand's Tasman Glacier). Running them close came electronics, scuba diving and photography. Ideally each person would be master of as many of these skills as possible. For the rest, character was what counted most of all, best judged by personal experience in the wilderness. 'General purpose' expeditioners, all of us, in fact, must be Jacks or Jills of all trades — from seacook to scientific field assistant. Sailing experience, while highly desirable, I did not consider essential for everyone. The Southern Ocean would soon enough turn greenhorns into seamen.

There was one person who in himself fulfilled just about every possible criterion for inclusion. This was Colin Putt. It was a bitter disappointment when his firm absolutely forbade him to go; he was urgently needed to reorganise a foundering factory. Colin did his best to hide his disappointment. Not only had he done more than anyone else to prepare the expedition but, more to the point, his qualifications as an ice pilot, polar mountaineer, skilled engineer and his staunch character added up to something unique. Near irreplaceable as he was, we had no alternative but to do our best without him.

Our best turned out to be very good indeed — in the person of Lars Larsen, that veteran of Greenland and Antarctica who, as already mentioned, I chose as my second-in-command. Combining as he did the skills of diesel mechanic, professional radio operator, Baltic yachtsman and polar explorer, he was one of the mainstays of the expedition. Good-natured, quietly humorous and immensely competent, he was generally to be found at this time head down beside the engine, surrounded by tools and spare parts, muttering feelingly in Danish each time his blond Viking beard dipped into the oily bilge.

The two scientists chosen for the enterprise were Dr Pieter Arriens and Dr Peter Donaldson. The field of the former encompassed geology in general, the collection of oriented rock samples (to study the earth's magnetism), weather recording and radio operation. He was studying for his amateur radio operator's examination, which he passed with flying colours. *Solo* was thus able to link up with the world-wide Ham radio network — for which we had reason to be grateful to Pieter and his colleagues of the air.

Dr Peter Donaldson, the other scientist, came late in the day with strong recommendations from Fritz Schaumberg and the other Pieter. Though a research chemist at the Australian National University, he was also a biologist whose main study had been the birds of northern Canada. In addition, he was an experienced mountaineer who had taken part in three of Sir Edmund Hillary's expeditions as film sound recorder. Peter's main responsibilities aboard *Solo* were to study the water chemistry around icebergs, to organise systematic bird and whale counts, to collect biological specimens and to do the sound recording for the ABC film. My only concern was his lack of sea experience so I insisted on a trial sail. Unfortunately this took place in sheltered waters and failed to reveal Peter's unsuspected vulnerability to seasickness.

Jack Pittar we had met in Darwin of all unlikely places. I was much impressed by the calibre of this unassuming young man who was an electronics technician with the department of National Mapping and had considerable deep sea experience. As a person, a seaman and an expert, Jack was to prove a very happy choice. Without his extraordinary flare for things electrical nothing in that line would have worked, once the damp and cold of the Southern Ocean had begun to take their toll. His successes included the autopilot, the log, the radios, many of the scientific instruments and ultimately the radar, not to mention such mundane but important things as electric lights and battery charging systems.

The proportion of two scientists (or three, if Jack be included) in an eight-man crew may seem small at first sight. In fact it is a good deal higher than on most Antarctic bases. One that I visited had two scientists and twenty-two support personnel — a more usual ratio.

New Zealander Dot Smith had been one of the 'Snowy mountaineers' in 1975. She and I were very old friends indeed, having climbed together in New Zealand in the far off pre-war days. Now a widow, Dot helps her son run their 1500-acre sheep farm on the rugged west coast of the North Island. She remains a member of the New Zealand Alpine Club and recently went trekking in Peru and the Himalayas. At fifty-nine she was the second oldest aboard (I am her senior by a year), but she was hard as nails and proved to be as fit and tough as any of the young men in the crew — as I well knew she would. Dot was recruited as a 'general purpose' crew member. It was never intended that she should devote an undue proportion of her time to cooking.

The last of the three mountaineers in the party (and the most skilled) was Fritz Schaumberg. A noted skier and scuba diver besides, he was Canberra manager of the well-known sports goods store of Paddy Pallin. Fritz was an old Snowy Mountains companion of mine, whose wry sense of humour, especially when everything was going wrong, was a major asset. He had been talking about the Balleny Islands for years and had once made a very good try at persuading the Russians to drop him off there from a whaler. Negotiations broke down over the uncertainty of being able to pick him up.

'We *may* visit the Ballenys' I told him over the telephone, 'but there is no certainty at all because the pack ice will likely as not block them completely.' No more was needed.

'I will come' said Fritz, and he proceeded to organise our equipment in masterly fashion.

The last member of the crew was the ABC's representative, cameraman and acting film director Ted Rayment. A veteran of the *Big Country* television series, he was also the most technically competent yachtsman on *Solo*. By an extraordinary coincidence, Ted had been at the helm of *Gallivanter,* sister ship to *Ice Bird,* when she capsized in a hurricane-force storm off Coffs Harbour.

'Even if the boat is sinking, your job is to film' his former *Big Country* director insisted implacably. In retrospect, I realise that Ted's very expertise made it very difficult for him to follow this advice and remain detached. His achievement in making a first class film is all the more praiseworthy.

Though for the sake of convenience *Solo's* crew have all been listed here in one place, in reality they were never able to come together as a group.

Dot had to stay in New Zealand until a fortnight before our departure, Peter Donaldson was held up in Canberra even longer, while Fritz's and Pieter Arriens' visits to Sydney were necessarily fleeting. Even those staying locally had their own preparations to attend to (Ted Rayment, for instance, was fully occupied in obtaining equipment and film) and had little time to spare for the more general preparations. I was more concerned that we were never once able to sail together as a team prior to our final departure.

Without the tremendous efforts of our unpaid helpers, *Solo* could never have been got ready in six weeks from the date of her purchase. Apart from Colin Putt, two wonderful young English brothers, Jim and John Marland, literally lived aboard *Solo,* together with the South African yachtsman Graham Cox who had formerly performed a like service for *Ice Bird.* Yvonne was on the 'phone from morning to night. Particularly trying for her was the circumstance that her little home on Dangar Island was never empty of people, as many as a dozen staying there at one time. Welcome as these helpers were, their continual presence in a confined space did not make it any easier to organise. I too felt the strain not a little. So overwhelmed with necessary jobs was I that it was not until the very last moment that I could set aside an uninterrupted half day for so vital a task as sorting out charts and navigation tables.

It may seem that I am overstressing the fitting-out problems, seeing that *Solo* had been found to be essentially sound and in good order on a recent survey and was well equipped for long distance cruising. But the Southern Ocean is no ordinary sea and Antarctic waters are hazardous cruising grounds. All the following had to be done in those six weeks. Rope ratlines ('ladders' attached to the stays) were set up on one side as far as the lower spreaders. We reluctantly gave up the idea of a crow's nest, where the lookout could be protected from the weather, because it would have interfered too much with the rig. It is essential in pack ice to have a man aloft to con the ship through the leads. Our lookout would certainly get cold; he would have to be changed frequently. A strong steel cabin door was installed in place of the old wooden one. Steel shutters were fitted over the largest windows and emergency wooden shutters, that could be clamped over the smaller windows should they be stove-in, were stowed in a handy locker. A 'canvas' dodger was laced round the rails, loosened below so that water could readily pour off the deck. Safety wires, to which our safety belts could be clipped, were rigged along the deck. Graham constructed a false floor to the fore cabin for extra stowage, and also a storage bin and table for the radios and meteorological instruments. Meanwhile other helpers were painting the yacht a high visibility orange; a yachtswoman was repairing sails and another making canvas leeboards for the bunks (to prevent the occupants falling out). The large 'fridge was removed and the gas stove replaced by a kerosene pressure one, given us by the makers, Brandts. (Kerosene is more easily carried than bottled gas on long voyages; we actually put on board nearly 1000 litres in ten 100 litre drums, manhandled into the lazarette with difficulty and firmly dogged down with stout timbers. This was a year's supply.)

Work on the slip was held to a minimum to save expense. A steel stem piece was fitted to strengthen the bow against ice. A fitting for attaching an emergency steering chain was welded onto the rudder (rudders have become casualties in the pack before today). Certain skin fittings, notably the sink outlet, which would be under the waterline after loading, were blocked off. Topsides painting was completed and anti-fouling applied.

Solo was designated as a 'Selected Ship' by the Meteorological office, whereby elaborate observations of everything from cloud cover to water temperature had to be made every six hours, encoded and sent off by radio. The instruments lent us had to be installed as well as *Snow Petrel*, an oceanographic buoy with a satellite tracking device, that was lent by the Oceanography and Fisheries Division of the CSIRO. The two-metre-long buoy was firmly attached by steel straps spot-welded to the side decks. *Snow Petrel* was powered by solar cells and contained an antenna. At each passage of the appropriate satellite it radioed our position. This information was recorded in the United States and was passed on to Australia by letter. Only in special circumstances could we obtain information from *Snow Petrel* as to our current position, and then only via radio after several days. Its purpose was to enable us subsequently to pinpoint the location of any scientific observations made by *Solo* . In this the device proved invaluable. Not even when the solar panel was snow-covered did it fail to function.

Our long distance radios were two Stingray sets given to us by Maurice Findlay, the designer and manufacturer. Not content with this, the helpful Maurice worked side by side with Jack Pittar installing the sets. We had given him far too little notice of our needs so he had had crystals specially flown from Singapore. The last night before sailing Jack and Maurice worked the whole night through so that the installations should be as near perfect as possible and ready for inspection and licensing in the morning.

It is standard practice, especially in a steel vessel, to have the compass swung prior to any long voyage. I dispensed with this because we would be approaching the South Magnetic Pole where the earth's magnetic field would be nearer vertical than horizontal and the yacht's own magnetism far stronger than the distant North Pole's. The compass could be expected to deviate progressively as we sailed south and ultimately to fail altogether. In such circumstances any adjustments carried out in Sydney would be misleading later on.

If all this work was rather overwhelming, it was nothing compared with the task of obtaining food and equipment and organising further fund-raising activities. The brunt of this fell to Yvonne, who had recently broken her arm in an accident in the garden — of all unlikely places. No fewer than fifty-three firms donated their products — virtually all our food, medicines, major items like the Beaufort inflatable surf boat and a 25 hp Evinrude outboard motor to go with it. Beauforts agreed to service our own inflatable life raft that had come with *Solo*. However, it was so old that it disintegrated when inflated, so they put us further in their debt by lending us a new one.

By this time Yvonne had pestered radio and television stations so often that they generally agreed to her requests for interviews and time on shows to stop her nagging them. One such was the Mike Walsh television show

Facing page • *Solo* at anchor in Solo Harbour
Following pages • *top left* **Solo** *in action*   *top right* **Pieter Arriens reading met. instruments**
bottom **Peter Donaldson and Fritz mend sails**
top **Tabular iceberg** *bottom* **Christmas on *Solo***

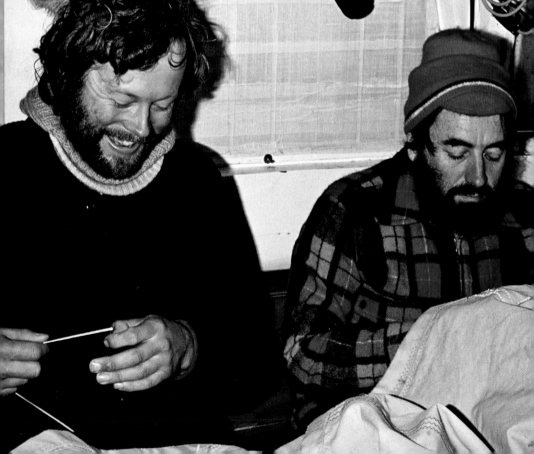

where the Beaufort surfboat and its motor were presented. Everything became rather mixed up; I am sure that the good ladies in the audience were left with the impression that we proposed to sail to the Antarctic in the little 'rubber duck'.

None of us was experienced in handling small boats in surf; if we were to avoid some chilly duckings during landings in Antarctica it was imperative that we have instruction. The Jack Wilson Motor Surf Lifesaving Club at Curl Curl kindly took us in hand. Lars and I duly turned up one afternoon with our 'rubber duck' on a borrowed pick-up to be initiated into the art. Lars was much quicker at learning the principles of timing the surf and reacting with split-second decisions than I. A lot more practice would have been desirable so that reflexes could become automatic but there simply was not time. I was to regret my lack of skill later.

The letter writing and telephoning that had to be done can be imagined. A word about publicity is in order because from the foregoing we do sound a little like 'publicity hounds'. We *had* to publicise our enterprise so that the public and industry, upon whom we perforce had to rely, should know about us. We would all much rather have gone about our preparations quietly and in private, relieved of the embarrassing need to blow our own trumpets. But we had not the resources without community support. In retrospect, I realise that the value of a private expedition like ours largely rested on the extent to which the public identified with our efforts. At the time this was not so easy to see.

Australia is not the easiest country in which to obtain cold-weather gear. Insulated rubber boots were the greatest problem. We were lent mukluks, and Dot, Pieter, Lars and I posessed our own, but these excellent warm boots are not waterproof enough to be worn on deck except in the calmest weather. The problem of clothing to protect against wet cold was a very real one. Fritz Schaumberg saved the day with Canadian insulated lumberjacks' boots, though these were never quite warm enough during the frigid hours standing in the open at the helm. Waterproof mitts and gloves, polar sleeping bags (synthetic filled, for down loses its insulation properties when damp), mountaineering gear, tents, skis, wet suits and much else we owed to Fritz. He proved an invaluable equipment officer.

This is not the place to list systematically our equipment, our supplies or our donors. The appendices and acknowledgments are more appropriate. Here only such items as have direct bearing on the story will be mentioned. Among these must rank the heavy weather waterproof clothing supplied by my old friends of *Ice Bird* days, Marlins. Then again, Philips' quartz crystal clock was an absolute boon for navigation. The Earth Sciences Department of Macquarie University brought us a compact winch that they had constructed for bottom sampling on the continental shelves. This was bolted in place to the cockpit coaming on the opposite side from *Snow Petrel*.

Finance remained a problem for such cash items as insurance, slipping, and so on (though, even here, we were given handsome concessions). Fitting out was interrupted for a week, therefore, while *Solo* was opened to the public at Circular Quay, Sydney Cove. We owed entirely to the kindness of the Maritime Services Board that we could bring the yacht virtually into the

Facing page • *top* **Patching the hole in *Solo's* hull**   *bottom* **An iceberg looms in front of Lars**

city centre for a week and set up tables on the quay side to sell T-shirts, *Ice Bird* books, raffle tickets and for an Antarctic photographic and equipment exhibition. The weather was blazing hot. Every now and then we took off along the pavements in bare feet in search of cool drinks or to make use of the welcome showers at the Unilever building across the road. I for one became sunburnt and bright pink. How we longed for the shade. But too much sunshine was not going to be a problem for long. This was a trying interlude in many ways, but it was redeemed by the warmth and friendliness of the public. This heartened us even more than the $1000 that was collected.

Originally it had been planned that each participant in the expedition should contribute $2000 as his share of the expenses. But since the aquisition of *Solo* came so late and the expedition was put together hurriedly, not all the crew could afford this sum and their contribution had to be wholly or partly in kind. Ted Rayment was in a separate category, since the ABC were paying his wages and the Foundation his overtime. This disparity between individuals' financial outlay should by rights have caused a certain amount of ill feeling, but it did not. Every one of the crew was keen and highly motivated and each was giving what he felt he could. Still, I think it advisable on our next expedition, prepared longer in advance, that strict uniformity should be the rule.

Another lesson for the future concerned the provision of free equipment. A tendency developed to take for granted that every item should be available without charge — as a kind of right. This seems anomalous when far more was given us than we ever anticipated. But it is human nature, when something has come for nothing, to expect more. A more sensible procedure in the future would be for lists of clothing and equipment to be provided for each member (as they were this time by Fritz) but on the clear understanding that each must purchase his own. Then any donation would be appreciated as a welcome windfall.

Back to Dangar Island we sailed for last minute alterations and loading. A year's food was to be carried, together with the 1000 litres of kerosene that would be needed to cook and melt ice and snow into drinking water. This very necessary precaution was in case of being frozen in and having to winter over. In that event our iron rations would be augmented by hunting. We would not be the first to survive in this way. After wintering at Cape Adare Campbell and Priestley's party were landed further down the Ross Sea coast. Ice prevented the ship from picking them up again and they spent the winter of 1912 in an ice cave, afterwards sledging 200 miles to safety. We did not anticipate any such mischance, but we had to be prepared and equipped to manage on our own. No one, in my opinion, should embark on the open ocean, the Antarctic, or any wilderness for that matter, not prepared to get out of trouble by his own efforts. By voluntarily challenging the elements he automatically assumes the responsibility for his own safety. He should not expect anyone to risk life and property on his behalf. The very idea of possible rescue is debilitating to the will; it should be replaced by self reliance.

Solo's rations were dehydrated or canned in the main. Many snacks were available that did not require cooking (a boon in bad weather or ashore): dried fruit, sweets, cracker biscuits, salami, corned beef. Fresh eggs and onions were carried and lasted very well. A butcher friend of Fritz's even gave us twenty kilos of fresh steak which we kept in 'Eskys' filled with dry ice; it lasted nine days. Such was the generosity of the many firms involved, and such were Yvonne's efforts that the Foundation had to pay only $411 for its year's food supply for eight people.

Fresh water would be obtainable from the ice, but not very conveniently. The water tanks held 912 litres and 544 litres more was carried in plastic drums lashed along the side decks, a total of 1456 litres. Strict water discipline was maintained on board so that, in the event, this supply sufficed for the whole voyage. The 1824 litres of diesel fuel in the tanks likewise proved adequate. In separate fuel tanks and cans on deck we carried outboard fuel, lubricating oil and petrol for the generator. Also on deck went the Beaufort inflatable, Fritz's Avon, a sledge-kyak (two kyaks connected by a framework — a sledge that would float), the Beaufort emergency life raft and the outboards.

Almost as important as food and fuel were books. Apart from navigational tables, instruction books and the like, *Solo's* library was made up of a good selection of polar classics, which we owed to Pieter Arriens, and a fair number of novels. These were a very great relaxation indeed; given more time to prepare I would have taken more still.

The day we loaded the food was a nightmare. A dozen or more helpers under Dot's command sorted it into plastic bags and stowed it aboard. The job was too much for one person to keep track of and the helpers gave up filling in the stowage book, with the result that it was a long time before we found where everything was. It was a miracle that nothing more than some of the peanut butter was left behind. Fortunately, the first week's supplies were in the ready-to-use lockers around the galley so there was time to sort out the rest in relative leisure. All told, *Solo* was carrying nine tonnes of stores and equipment.

The final departure was from Sydney Cove. We arrived from Dangar Island in the evening scheduled to sail at noon next day. While Jack Pittar and Maurice Findlay did their all-night marathon installing radios, the others were no sluggards. Exhausted with manhandling and stowing food and equipment, several helpers collapsed in the small hours, curled up on the sails on deck, and did not awaken until the film crews arrived in the early morning.

Morning brought no respite. The radios had to be inspected before our call sign VJ6764 could be approved. Pieter's Ham set was installed separately. The Customs duly cleared us, though they were not quite sure whether our destination counted as 'going foreign' or not. Now it was the turn of press, radio and television. Sir Adrian Curlewis drew our raffle. The irrepressible Dick Smith presented Yvonne with a ticket for an Antarctic flight that was due to pass over us, and went on to add a further donation. At the last minute we were all cheered by the advent of three cartons of Red Mill overproof rum. Then it was time for those heartrending goodbyes and that awful hollow feeling that comes when one stands on the brink of an adventure, and which passes once the battle is joined in earnest. At 12.30pm on December 15, 1977, half an hour later than planned, we cast off and motored out into the stream.

Sail was hoisted opposite the Opera House and *Solo* took off down the harbour at such a rate of knots that neither the accompanying ocean-racing yachts nor the ABC's film launch could keep up with her. Pausing only to heave-to to put off a camera crew, we rounded South Head at 1.30 pm, *Solo* came hard on the southerly wind and, rising and dipping to the ocean swell, headed in brilliant sunshine out over the blue white-flecked Pacific. Hard to believe, but we were really off at last.

Chapter 3

The Voyage South, How the Crew were Tempered

The handling of a yacht at sea comes down to some very simple essentials. First and always it is the wind that calls the tune. Your navigation, the periodic fixes with the sextant and the calculations of direction, speed and drift that make up dead reckoning, tells you where you are (or should do). You know where you want to go, south in our case. If the wind is favourable (fair or free) you sail in that direction. If, as is often the case, the wind is unfavourable, you put the yacht on the most advantageous tack, bearing in mind the likely wind shifts you anticipate.

The wind being east of south and *Solo's* needing to clear the coast, we found ourselves heading a little north of east, a circumstance which Fritz particularly found distressing. Not until 11 pm were we far enough offshore to tack with advantage. Coming round then to the port tack (the wind on the left hand or port side), we headed close-hauled down the coast roughly in the direction of Wollongong.

Apart from adapting its course to the wind's direction, a yacht must adjust its sail area to the wind's strength. *Solo* has no reef points in the mainsail so, in our case, the process boiled down to hoisting smaller or larger sails. *Solo's* headsails may for convenience be labelled in descending order of size the number 1, number 2, number 3 jibs and the storm jib. The first two set on twin forestays, the latter two one at a time on an inner stay. Next, moving aft, comes the mainsail, which may be replaced by a smaller storm trysail, then the mizzen on its separate mast behind the helmsman.

Solo rounded South Head under full cruising rig — number 1 jib, mainsail, and mizzen. As the wind increased in strength, the mizzen was first lowered, then hoisted again and the mainsail taken in and the number 1 jib replaced by a smaller. Before midnight the wind fell light and the mainsail and number 1 were re-hoisted. So raw a crew were we that this latter operation, what with reeling around the deck in the dark, mixing up winches and sheets, chilled by the spray that struck cold despite the 26°C air temperature, took us a full one and a half hours. Clearly our teamwork had a long way to go.

This was not unexpected since Dorothy, Fritz, Peter Donaldson and Jack

Pittar had very little yachting experience, while Pieter Arriens was stronger on theory than on practice. I split us up therefore into two watches, myself taking over the starboard watch, whose other members were Jack Pittar, Ted Rayment and Peter Donaldson. The practice of the skipper, especially if he is also the only navigator, having to stand regular watches is not a good one. His sun sights, generally taken in the morning and/or the afternoon and around noon do not fit in well with the rigid schedule. More important, he loses touch to some extent with half of the crew and tends to lose sight of overall strategy. There was no help for it in our case, and my hopes for a change were dashed by Ted's request a week or so later to be relieved of watch keeping so as to give him more flexibility for filming. He was right; a worthwhile film immeasurably complicates the work of any expedition, since many awkward activities (surf landing, for instance) have to be duplicated to get the right shots. I cursed Ted silently at the time, but he was justified by the result. The port watch was led by Lars Larsen and made up of Fritz, Dot and Pieter Arriens. With only two watches, we were four hours on and four off and so never had an unbroken sleep of more than about three hours. This unsatisfactory arrangement was born out of the need to train the crew. On the return journey we were able to adopt a far more comfortable three watch system.

Rules are best kept to a minimum at sea. We had only two. Safety belts were to be worn on deck or in the cockpit at all times at sea. Everyone followed this to the letter, in part I am convinced because the safety lines were simple and quick to tie round the waist. Elaborate shoulder harnesses, that are very difficult to put on over storm clothing and have to be removed just as laboriously at every call of nature, have no real advantage over a waist line such as generations of mountaineers have used. Much better a waist loop worn consistently for three months than a theoretically superior harness discarded after a week. The first principle of ocean sailing is to keep the crew aboard or, at any rate, firmly attached to the ship. A man adrift is not easy to spot or pick up at night or in big seas, nor does he remain afloat for very long in Antarctic temperatures.

A yacht at sea is most readily destroyed by fire. The risk was minimised by *Solo's* having a diesel-powered motor, all petrol for outboards et cetera being stowed on deck. Cooking too was by kerosene in place of the far more inflammable and explosive propane gas. Our second rule banned smoking from the bunks and cabin except for the two seats just inside the entrance. This precaution too was observed. Even so, with three heavy smokers aboard, the atmosphere below was not improved and I regretted the free cigarettes that had been provided. Never again.

Noon on the second day found us racing along at eight and nine knots with the wind abeam. But the fair breeze did not last; it soon died away and, when it freshened again, it did so violently and from ahead. This was a good day, nevertheless. A noon sight put us off Jervis Bay, eighty-four miles south of Sydney Heads (our runs were measured between noon positions without allowance for deviations due to tacking. The day's run 'through the water' would have been a good deal further but not all in the right direction). The land was a hazy line to starboard.

'If we did not know where we were from David's sight — that is if he has not been kidding us' Lars remarked, 'we would know we could only be near

Australia because of the flies.' He brushed ineffectively at the cloud of insects that were swarming around him and continued cutting up fresh steak for the evening meal.

'Where is the funnel for filling the stove?' Ted called plaintively. Alas, it had been forgotten. The previous night had revealed that there was no large flashlight either. Not bad so far — a lot more items could have been overlooked in all the rush. Not long after that one of the buckets was lost overboard — the first casualty.

At 5.30 pm (Eastern Summer Time, Sydney time, was used throughout the voyage; the course was not very much east of south and communication with Australia and the Australian bases was facilitated), a gale-force southerly squall, heralded by a black escarpment of cloud, had all hands hurriedly shortening sail and being soaked by rain and spray in the process.

Dot heroically cooked the first main meal of the voyage in a wild steep sea that sent her lurching across the cabin and anything unsecured on the table flying. Dot apparently never suffered from seasickness and seemed to be made of rubber, for more times than I can remember she was flung against a bulkhead. She never quite came to terms with the ship's motion by learning to anticipate what was likely to happen but, beyond a lot of bruises, she did not come to serious harm. Her stew was a very good one.

A rather miserable night, as the wind slackened leaving behind a sickening lop, was followed by an equally trying morning, during which short steep seas and an erratic head wind impeded our progress. The day began with Lars going aloft up the mizzen mast to free a fouled halyard. My morning inspection showed that several drums along the side decks had shifted. We painstakingly re-lashed them and they gave no further trouble. By evening our little world had changed out of all recognition. A freshening north-easter, that gusted periodically up to gale force, sent us bowling along, the seas racing alongside, pouring white over the side decks and filling the sheeting well behind the cockpit. Between the scudding clouds appeared the waxing moon; then the Southern Cross, high above the port shrouds. The steel cabin door was kept closed all night lest a boarding sea flood the cabin. Dot and Ted managed to concoct a hot stew. 'Now we all are beginning to get the "feel" of the sea; the mood aboard is happy and exhilarated' I wrote in my diary. It is times like these that make ocean cruising worthwhile.

From the outset of the voyage Pieter Arriens initiated six-hourly meteorological observations and continued them conscientiously until the last. He had to note the wind direction and strength, the state of the sea and the nature and extent of the cloud cover; the wet and dry bulb thermometers in the little white box in the mizzen rigging were read and the sea water temperature taken. The results were encoded for transmission and sent off to Melbourne. The conversation went like this.

Pieter: 'Hallo Sydney radio, hallo Sydney radio, hallo Sydney radio. This is *Solo, Solo, Solo.* This is Victor Juliet 6764, *Solo.* Come in please. Over.'

Sydney radio: 'Victor Juliet 6764, *Solo.* I have you strength three. Over.'

Pieter: 'I have a ship's wireless weather report for you. May I transmit it on 4125 Mhz?'

Sydney radio: 'Affirmative. Go ahead *Solo.*'

Pieter: 'Weather report for Meteo Melbourne. Our serial number fourteen, twelve groups, reading as follows.' (The code numbers are now transmitted in twelve groups.) 'End of message' Pieter would conclude. 'How do you copy? Over.'

Sydney radio: 'All received your serial number fourteen. Thank you *Solo*. Sydney radio. Out.'

Pieter: 'Thank you Sydney radio. This is *Solo*. Out.'

Not always by any means was reception as clear as this. Messages had to be repeated time and again and no praise is too high for the patience of the Australian coastal radio stations and later the Antarctic base operators, nor yet for the methodical and persistent Pieter. It detracts not at all from his stalwart efforts that the messages were immediately swallowed up in the anonymity of the Meteorological Office's computer.

At this early stage of the voyage the first failure of electronic equipment came to plague us. The autopilot began to develop a most erratic will of its own. I suspect that the radar too, which had been working very well at the outset, but which we were to have no further occasion to use until the first icebergs were encountered, went quietly to sleep about this time. Jack Pittar plunged at once into the autopilot's innards, dismantling its compass and magnets and crawling over food bags in the lazarette to get at the motor and gearing. By afternoon the invaluable gadget was in operation again.

'By the way, what shall we call it?' someone asked.

'George' was the first suggestion.

'Fred' said Jack firmly.

'Jack is his friend, so he has the right to name him' I adjudicated. So Fred the autopilot remained. He was too heavy on current to use in light winds. But at anything over six knots under sail the free-wheeling propellor generated sufficient electricity to operate Fred or, of course, when the motor was running.

Solo worked her way southward in erratic changeable weather, though the prevailing winds as expected in these latitudes, were from the south-west. These winds had the effect of pushing us a good deal to the eastward of our direct track until by the end of the first week we were well over towards the New Zealand side of the Tasman Sea and a little south of Tasmania. Progress had not been bad, totalling 704 miles, the best twenty-four hours' run having been 126 miles. It was appreciably colder. The crew had settled into the rhythm of the passage and were learning their trade pretty fast. The tough mountaineer Fritz was not well, suffering the first of a series of low grade but irritating virus infections that were to worry him for several weeks. Peter Donaldson was badly affected by seasickness, but never a watch did he miss. He would literally crawl out into the cockpit a pale green colour and sit there semi-comatose until a call came for action. Then he would stagger blindly to the mast and haul, as often as not, on the wrong rope. I have rarely witnessed such stubborn courage. All my instincts were to send him below, but I knew that his superhuman efforts were the only way to get the better of his sickness so let him carry on. His determination was rewarded. Slowly but steadily his health improved, leaving him eight kilos lighter but fit again and, what is more, an efficient seaman.

Accounts of expeditions can never be the same since the publication of that classic, *The Ascent of Rum Doodle,* by WE Bowman. This account of

40

the climb of a mythical mountain unmercifully flays the 'all good chaps' school of expedition reporting that too often covers up the real life human qualities of the participants and so denigrates their achievements. Take the following passage, for instance:

> Burley ... expressed the opinion that a scientist on an expedition was even more of a nuisance than his gear, which was considerable. He told us about his friend Groag, who shared a tent with a scientist on the 1923 expedition to Tum Teedle. Like all scientists, this one was very absent-minded. One day he inadvertently made tea with copper-sulphate solution instead of water, with the result that he and Groag turned blue and were colour-blind for a fortnight, being unable to distinguish blue from white. One day this scientist stepped off the edge of a snowfield thinking the blue sky beyond a continuation of the snow. He was saved only by great effort and devotion on the part of Burley, who had the misfortune to be roped to him. Burley said that any ordinary man would have left him to his fate.
>
> Wish said that he did not believe one word of the story. He himself had drunk gallons of copper-sulphate tea with impunity. The blue effect was no doubt due to cardio-synthesis of the bloodstream due to the rarefied atmosphere. He strongly resented the statement that all scientists were absent-minded. (The contestants, together with other members of the expedition, then resort to blows; the leader, with a mastery of cliches, sums up the evening.) ... no doubt that such little differences of opinion as might appear between us were evidence of the commendable frankness and openness with which we regarded one another, and that I had no reason to suppose that we would not make an efficient and united team.

Well I have no intention of going back to 'pre *Rum Doodle*' days. Apart from any other cause of irritation, we had found by experience that no more than five bunks plus the starboard cabin settee were really usable at sea. The homeless ones, Jack, myself and either Peter Donaldson or Ted, had to use whoever's bunk happened to be unoccupied. We were the worst off, having no one place belonging to us where we could stow our clothing and possessions. But the permanently settled were disadvantaged too. Everyone needs a private corner to himself, where he can turn to the wall and pretend for a while that no one else is there. He also needs a niche of his own where his things will remain undisturbed. The lack of individual bunks, plus the fact that we were eating, cooking, radioing, navigating, making notes and sleeping all in the one room, placed considerable strain on everyone's good nature. Without wishing to sound like the bumbling leader in *Rum Doodle* I must say that all showed remarkable self-control.

Our diaries provided an outlet, and I fear that my own short-comings were the butt of a good deal of no doubt well-merited criticism. Here is Peter Donaldson.

> Lars and I keep up a good-natured banter with each of us playing jokes on the other. I tried to get him up yesterday to see an Antarctic Rosella but he didn't move and I only caught Dot.
>
> David seems happier the worse the weather becomes. He resembles a pirate or vulture perched out at the helm. I've asked him not to scare

away my birds as he looks so grotesque with his ratty old hat, a wild look in his eye and a maniacal grin creasing his snow-covered face (this was written two weeks further on).

I really enjoy working with Jack on deck. The two of us are partners in adversity as we have great trouble in understanding David's vague commands. Often we get wet, cold and furious when he keeps ploughing head on into big seas whilst we change sails up for'ard. When we abuse him, he just smiles and waves — he can't hear a thing through his hat. Lars and the rest of us turn briefly downwind for sail changes and everyone remains a lot drier.

Personal idiosyncrasies become irritating. Peter Donaldson again.

Dot's voice driving me mad . . . Dot is also doing some steering and now, having something to do and being more tired, is much easier to live with.

In fact Peter and Dot got along together particularly well, having much in common with their experiences in the Himalayas.

Peter's remarks about my vagueness recall inescapably Lewis Carroll's *The Hunting of the Snark.*

He was thoughtful and grave — but the orders he gave
Were enough to bewilder the crew.
When he said 'Steer to starboard,
But keep her head larboard,'
What on earth was the helmsman to do?

I hope I was not this bad!

Once clear of Tasmania the seas grew bigger and more irregular; the motion violent. 'You need to grow long fingernails to hang onto your bunk,' the irrepressible Fritz put it. Three years out of practice, I was finding difficult the taking of sextant sights from a low tossing platform from which the horizon was only momentarily visible from the wave crests and the sun like as not obscured by cloud at the crucial second. Gradually the art came back to me, though I am sure that Fritz for one regarded it with deep suspicion as a kind of black magic, judging by his relieved astonishment when we at last made our intended landfall. Once I had regained my confidence, I began teaching astro-navigation to those who were interested. Lars was a particularly quick learner. Before we crossed the Antarctic Circle he had taken over the noon observations entirely and was soon competant to handle the other more complicated calculations as well. Peter Donaldson followed in Lars' wake and had begun to play his part in the navigation before the voyage was over. Pieter Arriens tried but was never quite able to grasp the mathematics of the thing, nor did his onerous radio schedules leave him much time for extraneous study.

All this time Jack and Pieter Arriens had been hard at work installing Pieter's own Ham radio. Now it worked perfectly and contact was made with Davis Base, of which Pieter had been leader the year before, and where my old friend Col Christiansen was radio operator. Pieter was in his element. Before long he was in contact with a whole network of amateur operators in Australia, thanks to whom we were soon in regular touch with Yvonne. This was important, not just to me, but to be sure of channelling accurate news of our progress to the media. There had already been one garbled report published to the effect that we were 'two hundred miles off course'. This can only have been a misunderstanding of the fact that head winds had forced us to the east. Now, thanks largely to a Ham operator, Barry White of Sydney, all information passed through Yvonne's hands. I was very relieved once this system was working well, because the confused reports that appear about ocean yachtsmen have to be seen to be believed. I myself have been 'lost with all hands' once, been 'missing' often and, on one glorious occasion, reported as having been 'eaten by South American Indians'. It sometimes seems as if the term 'missing' applied to yachtsmen is as much a cliché as 'intrepid' for mountaineers.

A shout from Lars at the helm electrified the innocents below.

'Has anybody here seen a whale before?' When most of the crew had rushed on deck and stared round the empty horizon, Lars explained, mock innocent, 'I only wanted to know. I did not mean there *was* one!' Next day we did see our first whale blowing in the distance. Peter Donaldson sighted it and at first nobody would believe him. This was a calm day so I was able to check the compass error accurately. It was increasing appreciably. Suddenly out of nowhere a small figure appeared porpoising by. The half-grown fur seal passed very near but took no notice whatsoever of *Solo*. It continued undeviating on its way, arching rhythmically out of the water until it was lost to view over the horizon.

The first week at sea was a particularly important time for all of us, for it was the crucial shake-down period when we began to work together as a team. It was too vital a period to be left to my pen alone to describe. We have seen some of Peter Donaldson's feelings. Here is Dot on the chaos of the first days at sea.

There is lots of confusion on board and equipment everywhere still without a place to live. I guess we'll get shipshape in due course. All tired and dropping off to sleep all over the place. Hard to stay awake on four-hourly watches . . . I have a good bunk, used by various bods while I am on watch.' But already by next day: 'Gradually a ship routine has emerged in not easy conditions, owing to the work load of various crew. Pieter A. has to read the weather forecasts four times a day, then Peter D. and I are doing the bird identification and count four times daily for ten minutes. I guess I'll soon learn something of birds in time. I'm doing most of the cooking at present but have had lots of help from Fritz and Ted, then several wash up or clear away the rubbish . . . I felt seasick for two days when below and actually vomited a tiny bit. The seas have been quite rough with two days of gale force winds, David commended me on being able to produce a reasonable meal . . .

So he should have, indeed! Dot was proving herself a real sea heroine.

The fine sunny day at the end of the first week was a relief to Dot as it was to all of us.

Saw hundreds of prions (ice birds) today and I am sure they are feeding above acres of fish. A lovely lone fur seal came to visit us before dinner and spent twenty minutes dancing round the ship, often cleaning his flippers and bouncing out of the water. Then a superb sunset and flat sea gave us all a lot of pleasure . . . Have to be careful of the water, do all cooking in salt water in pressure cookers.

Dot goes on to comment on a missed radio sked:

> . . . poor Peter A. was asleep and was furious that no one thought to waken him. He is so serious about it all, what would happen if we overturned or our radio cut out? . . . Made two batches of scone mix, well received, but I'd rather have my own mixture. Later there was a general shifting of radio batteries, sewing sails, mending . . . I have bruises everywhere from knocking against all sorts of things. Catapulted into Fritz's lap from across the counter to-day, nearly destroyed him.

Chafing of ropes, especially sheets, and of the stitching of synthetic sails is the chief curse of long-distance cruising. A moment's slackening of vigilance and the seam of a sail, rubbing unnoticed against a wire shroud, will part. All our sails appeared to have become vulnerable at once early in the second week. A minor tear in the number two jib was followed by the opening of a very long seam in the number one — both on December 23. Despite feeling ill, Fritz volunteered to act the part of seamstress and started stitching the heavy Terylene with sail needle and palm. At two the next morning a great jagged tear appeared without warning in the mainsail. We lowered it at once and hoisted the mizzen and *Solo* continued to make seven knots.

With the coming of daylight on Christmas Eve we got to work. The mainsail was taken below to be repaired at some later date when opportunity offered. In its stead the small, very stout and heavy storm trysail was hoisted. We had just passed the 1000 mile mark and were about to leave astern away to the east Stewart Island, New Zealand, the southernmost land of consequence apart from Patagonia. More than half way through the Roaring Forties and approaching the Furious Fifties as we were, we considered that the storm trysail would be quite big enough in place of the far larger mainsail. This proved correct; the little trysail functioned admirably until replaced by the repaired Main only shortly before our arrival back in Sydney.

The mainsail apart, Fritz had taken on a very big job indeed. He became dizzy from eye strain in the reeling cabin and his hands got very sore, so that he had to stop and rest at intervals — for which he quite unnecessarily apologised! When the jibs were finally repaired next day the gallant Fritz had worked a total of eight hours.

All of us had been sending and receiving Christmas telegrams and messages for the past few days. This had only been possible through the persistence of Pieter Arriens, his Hams and the coastal stations, for radio reception was not good at the time. Christmas Day itself was a gay occasion. The Father Christmas brought by Lars, our penguin mascot made by the nursing sister at Dangar Island and the paper decorations Dot had brought were festooned around the cabin in a colourful array. The first two real penguins ignored us but a seal peered at us benignly as we passed, as if welcoming us into his domain. Thanks to Fred the autopilot we were able to sit down to dinner together, a sumptuous repast of Plumrose ham, mashed dehydrated potatoes and tinned salad, accompanied by a concoction of rum and coffee that Dot mixed in a bucket, Pieter's champagne and some well-wishers' whisky. We were all a little pensive, thinking of home — and what lay ahead.

What a contrast this was, I thought, to the two Christmases I had spent aboard the little ten-meter *Ice Bird*.* Five years since I had been alone. I was en route then towards the Antarctic Peninsula, the portion of the continent opposite South America 6000 miles south-east of Sydney, in the course of the first (and so far the only) single-handed voyage to Antarctica. Two weeks earlier *Ice Bird* had been hurled over and upside-down by a twenty-metre breaker in a hurricane-force gale, smashing mast, self steering gear, splitting the steel cabin top and leaving me frostbitten 3600 miles out from Sydney and 2500 from the Antarctic Peninsula, not far from the furthest point from land in any ocean. A week later *Ice Bird* was capsized again. I had not expected to survive. But then I had managed to work out a way of erecting the short but stout boom as a little mast and hoisting a makeshift rig upon it. On Christmas Day 1972 I had been able to write

'Rather dubious sun sights, the first for ten days, gave our (*Ice Bird* and me) position as 61°.30′S, 104°.57′W (this was real progress at last). If only these figures are correct this is ... the best Christmas present.' It certainly had been that, for there was then a sporting chance of my reaching Antarctica alive.

The following Christmas (1973) had seen *Ice Bird,* having been laid up for the winter at the American Antarctic base of Palmer, hove-to in fog off the bleak ice cliffs that guarded the Russian base of Bellingshausen. There had been no danger that time but a good deal of irritation with the fog that had frustrated my intention of visiting the base. Then I had been alone. Now our little isolated world was crowded — too crowded for comfort. I tried to compare my feelings on the two voyages.

I remembered what I had written about the time when survival had seemed doubtful. 'I was at least spared this desolate emotion (loneliness). My little drama was being played out on the vast stage of the Southern Ocean with death lurking in the wings, but my solitude, while full of anguish, was never lonely.'

The place of real loneliness is among people from whom you are set apart, as a stranger in an unfeeling big city, for instance. The solitude of the great peaks, deserts and oceans is not unfriendly, simply neutral and indifferent. Having said this, I must admit that by the end of the *Ice Bird* voyage in Capetown (or rather of my part in it — my son, Barry, took over and carried on to Sydney) my self-sufficiency had broken down. I had often sailed with companions and would do so again, but I would never have the mental stamina to make another voyage alone.

In a very real sense, however, I was more alone than ever aboard *Solo.* This was the solitude of command. There were undercurrents from the first as our different personalities interacted and our individual needs and peculiarities were thrown into relief by forced propinquity in confined quarters. Hopes, fears and goals were as varied as the people concerned. These were no dull automatons but intelligent and imaginative human beings who would react best to reasoned leadership. Yet sometimes, paradoxically, the utmost firmness would be required, for neither the Southern Ocean nor the Antarctic are tolerant of academic debate.

I was obsessed always with questions of whether or not to intervene.

---

* *Ice Bird,* Collins, London, 1975

Good-natured banter might imperceptibly slide into spitefulness; over-dedication to a person's own tasks could involve insensitivity to the needs of others — and so on. Hour after hour I would lie awake in my bunk (or rather, my borrowed one) worrying over each little set of problems. In general it usually seemed best to let things sort themselves out, sometimes aided by a discreet word or a change in routine. Rarely was I forced to lay down the law.

Was I doing the right thing? Was I explaining my reasons well enough? (I think not. As Peter Donaldson says, I tend to be vague.) There was no one to turn to for advice, and this was as it should be — at once the privilege and the responsibility of command. Above all, I must never ever take sides and I must do all in my power to prevent factions from developing. The realisation came as a surprise and not all at once, that I was more alone than I had been on *Ice Bird,* for now the lives of others were in my keeping. The ultimate responsibility for safeguarding them was mine and I was only too well aware of my own fallibility. Demanding as it was, I welcomed the challenge.

Barely was this 1977 Christmas over than signs heralding the end of the good weather anticyclone we had been enjoying began to appear. The barometer fell steadily; feathery mares' tails of cirrus cloud in the west spread and thickened into an opalescent haze and then into low ragged cloud, from which an icy rain began to fall; the north-west wind increased steadily to gale force. This was the warm front of a depression. The centre of low pressure that was causing the disturbance would be about south-west of us now and moving south-east at thirty knots or so (an important meteorological law states that if you face the wind in the Southern Hemisphere the centre of low pressure is 8 to 12 points, 92° to 137°, to your left. The wind being from the north-west this would put the centre of the low about south-west or south).

We could anticipate in this part of the Southern Ocean that, as the glass bottomed and began to rise, the sky would clear and the cold front be heralded by a backing to the west or west-north-west, perhaps by a vicious line squall. Further eastward in the Southern Ocean and to the north, the cold front wind (often gale) would be from the south-west. I can only speculate that the peculiarity of the wind directions south of Australia might be due to deflection by the continent.

The wind shift did not come till next evening when it arrived in a squall. 'Just gone through a red light,' exclaimed Fritz who was feverish again and on antibiotics, and so should not have been so cheerful. Incidentally, lest I seem to claim too much credit for weather prediction, the information cited above is almost all to be found set out in the *Antarctic Pilot.* True we were not yet in the waters covered by this admirable publication, these waters being those south of 60°S and 'southward of the usual route of vessels', but at 51° we were fast getting there.

We were indeed, I thought, as I took the helm that evening, muffled up in fur hat and Antarctic mitts. Then at the sheer beauty of the scene my trivial worries fled away. The near full moon was rising out of the sea astern and the whole southern half of the horizon in front was painted scarlet and gold by the late sunset. A solitary storm petrel, a jet black silhouette, went darting by across the bow.

Another day and another depression; then more lows in quick succession. We were having ample opportunity to perfect our sail changing. I had been worried about Ted's reluctance to get on with filming, but he suddenly got into his stride, filming the most traumatic sail changes, when white water went thundering down the side decks and flogging sails were overmastered only with difficulty. Once, in a fifty knot line squall, I had to rush out to the helm undressed and was duly soaked, though more fortunate than Fritz, who was completely immersed as the lee deck went under. Fritz removed his waterlogged boots, that he had labelled 'port' and 'starboard' and remarked cheerfully 'You know, Skipper, I should mark it on my feet too to remember'. Having changed, he began patiently stitching the mainsail.

But Fritz was not always well enough to take over the helm and, in the big seas we were encountering, the wheel kicked so violently that it was generally beyond Dot's strength to control. To make matters worse, Fred, the autopilot, was ailing again and not even his friend Jack could fix him. In retrospect, I realise that Fred's compass was beginning to feel the effects of the still distant South Magnetic Pole. One day when Fritz had lain apparently moribund in his bunk for hours, he unexpectedly asked for some soup. Ted, who was stirring away, was startled.

' I thought you were labelled "not wanted on voyage" ' he commented.

Peter Donaldson had got over his seasickness more or less completely by this time and he and Jack were fast becoming fully competent seamen. Lars, of course, had never been anything else. Pieter Arriens, whose minor brushes with just about every other member of the crew had worried me more than a little, unselfishly took over a good many of Fritz's watches. Ted also began to fill in to give Peter Donaldson, Jack or me a welcome break.

The close of the second week found us, after a record noon to noon run of 185 miles (this was never surpassed), another 800 miles on our way. We had passed some 120 miles west of Macquarie Island. We were south of it now, nearly 1500 miles south of Sydney. Only Cape Horn, a third of the way round the world, lay between us and Antarctica and it was only thirty miles to the south. At 55°.33'S we were well into the Furious Fifties, which were living up to their name.

Radio reports of the bad weather that the competitors in the Sydney-Hobart yacht race were encountering more than a thousand miles to the north, and which was forcing many retirements, rather amused us. This was hardly fair because, although the seas we were traversing were far more stormy than those around Tasmania, we were sailing Solo very gently, deliberately undercanvassed most of the time to safeguard our gear (for there were no replacements or outside assistance available to us). In ocean racing, on the other hand, nothing is spared; yachts and their crews are driven to the limit and so failures are inevitable.

More and more Dot was taking over the galley. This had never been intended and, looking back, I should have seen what was happening and forestalled it. Partly to blame was the circumstance that, barely had Dot become confident at the helm, when the seas became too rough for her to take the wheel very often. Then, in another respect, she herself was to blame, because she insisted on taking over whenever anyone else was cooking and became so possessive about 'her kitchen' that Ted and Fritz, her fellow cooks at the outset, were literally driven away. The development of this situation was understandable. Inexcusable is the shameful fact that Dot was often left with the washing up and cleaning chores as well. Pieter Arriens and Jack Pittar to their credit remained Dot's most consistent helpers. The rest of us have less reason to be proud. Not surprisingly, there is rather a plaintive note in the following account by Dot.

Making pikelets in force 9 gales can be quite a feat. I made hundreds of them to be devoured almost immediately by the waiting gannets (all male). I also made bread which I took to bed with me in my sleeping bag in a wobbly plastic basin for the dough to rise. It took about two hours and only once tipped upside-down. Then, placed in the pressure cooker without the pressure knob, it made quite good bread. The men had an uncanny sense of waking just as the bread came out of the pressure cooker and never once did it get cold before it was all gone.

Washing dishes on deck in freezing seawater is no joke but something which I did many times daily. One or two of the men did help, but usually when the engine was running, giving warm water. Washing ourselves was all done in cold seawater, so very little got done. I would strip off once a week in the forepeak, sitting on the toilet, but as this is the roughest part of the ship I often hit the roof or landed in a cold heap amongst my clothes.

However, I never went on watch without first washing my face, doing my hair and putting on lipstick, something which I think was secretly appreciated by most of the men.

This last point of Dot's is particularly important to my way of thinking. I have always regarded the 'outdoors he-man' mystique as something of a joke. Surely, now that New Zealand's Naomi Jacobs has beaten Chichester's record sailing solo round the world, it can be allowed to die a natural death! Women are quite capable of doing anything that men can do if they want to and are given the opportunity. What they lack in ultimate physical strength they make up in superior resistance to heat and cold. The Antarctic to a great extent still remains a stronghold of male exclusiveness, the two arguments most often advanced in its favour being the sexual tensions alleged to arise in mixed parties and toilet facilities.

My own experience with women companions in the mountains, the Australian desert, the grim waters off Tierra del Fuego and the Cape of Storms has been that their presence makes of a party a far more balanced human group. Society normally comprises both sexes and an all-male group is a socially ill-balanced one. As to tensions, these may arise in any grouping, never more violently than in all-male groups; and sex is hardly at a premium in the polar oceans and lands — the Ballad of Eskimo Nell notwithstanding. But I think that Dot should have the last word.

Being the only woman on board was interesting in many ways (she wrote after our return). I think there could have been some serious rows if I had not been there; as it was tempers flared only for a short time.

We had so many laughs and those are the times one remembers. As there were eight of us for only six bunks, it became a practice for the men

Facing page • *top* **David Lewis at the helm**   *bottom* **Buckle Island in the Ballenys**
Following pages • *top* **Sturge Island coastline**   *bottom* **A growler**
top ***Solo*** **at anchor in Solo Harbour**   *bottom* **The Beaufort beached at Sabrina Island**

to say: 'Dot, can I have your bunk?' They said my bunk smelt nice. Was it because of the lingering smell of yeast, or that I had done a little washing, I wonder?

There is a lot of underlying wisdom in Dot's remarks.

The argument that if women were allowed on Antarctic bases (as they have been on the Russian and New Zealand ones for years) separate toilet and other facilities would have to be constructed at great expense is simply not reasonable. In the first place, at least one country, often regarded as the most civilised in Western Europe, has never had time for such refinements even in its cities. In the second, when people are united in a common enterprise, as on a mountain climb or as in Dot's case, they readily learn to take any little embarrassments in their stride. This having been said, Dot *did* have a lot to put up with at times. We did little to spare her blushes.

'Dot, look quick!' calls Fritz from the helm. Dot scrambles into the cockpit in all innocence, only to find that the sight was Ted relieving himself over the rail. Unkind perhaps, but not unreasonable.

Dot's presence certainly mitigated the crudities of an all-male group a little, but not enough to turn the atmosphere into that of a Sunday School picnic — and that was just as it should be.

Dot was quick to comment upon the preoccupation with bodily functions that developed as the sea became more stormy and our clothing ever more cumbersome. The preoccupation was excusable seeing how difficult it was becoming for men to solve a problem analagous to getting two inches of frigid piping through six inches of lagging. Of course, for Dot, confined to the wildly gyrating forepeak, the problem was very much worse. Not that I did not have difficulties of my own. The slight enlargement of the prostate inseparable from my age dictated that I obey calls of nature relatively frequently and without delay. I was thus the main user of the pee bucket which was propped conveniently just outside the cabin, where the user did not risk a drenching. After a time the plastic bucket disintegrated — some alleged from the effects of strong acid, I maintained because of age — and a large jam tin was substituted.

One day when the tin had become battered and rusty I emerged sleepily from the cabin to come on watch to find Ted, Jack and Peter in the cockpit and an atmosphere of expectation that you could cut with a knife.

'Look what we have got for you, skipper, a new pee tin!' said Ted with unconvincing goodwill. Even in my sleepy state my suspicions were aroused as I took the shiny new tin Ted handed me. There had to be a catch. Fortunately I found it before making use of the attractive receptacle. The bottom had been neatly cut out!

Strong westerly winds and short-lived gales speeded us on our way. The runs of 113 miles, 138, 140 were encouraging. On December 30 we crossed the Antarctic Convergence in 58°S, where the cold Antarctic water moving up from the south sinks down below the warmer temperate water masses, and the sea temperature dropped abruptly to 4.7°C. The same day the first snow fell. We had not missed by much having a 'white Christmas' in southern mid-summer. There were no real night watches now, the sky

Facing page • *top left* **Dot Smith plays with a Weddell seal at Solo Harbour** *centre left* **A snow petrel stays overnight on** *Solo* *bottom left* **Bottom-sampling gear** *right* *Solo* **anchored in Solo Harbour**

merely darkened into a sort of twilight that lasted from 10 or 11 pm until 3 or 4 am. Before long even this limited dusk would disappear and the white Antarctic nights set in.

On New Year's Eve it was snowing heavily. Clumsy mitts were a necessity now, even for short tasks on deck. I slipped on the snow and fell over in the cockpit. It was now that the clothing listed by Fritz, and often obtained by him, came into its own. The long hours steering were the worst ordeal, made no easier because the steering compass was growing increasingly sluggish and Fred was hardly functioning at all. Each person's clothing varied somewhat, of course, in accordance with conditions and taste, but mine would be about average: nylon briefs, long cellular or quilted dacron underpants, cellular vest, New Zealand wool mountain shirt, heavy wool jersey, jeans, wool socks, insulated rubber gum boots or mukluks, thick quilted synthetic over-trousers, thick synthetic quilted parka, wool gloves or mitts with waterproof overmitts or industrial rubber gloves, or Antarctic 'nose wiper' mitts in dry conditions (eg steering, if not too rough), fur hat, ski goggles, when steering in driving snow, Marlin waterproof jacket and trousers in any but calmest weather, safety belt. Not surprisingly, a person coming on watch had to be called a full twenty minutes before coming on duty, and we did not take all those layers off in our sleeping bags!

Alternatives were New Zealand oilskins, Balaklavas (in place of what I will always maintain was an elegant fur hat. Once when I came below with it wet and bedraggled someone asked unkindly, 'Is that something you have just shot?'). There were windproof Ventile trousers, mainly for wearing on shore, sandshoes and, of course, changes of everything. Several of the party had climbing and ski boots, and there were tents, ice axes, climbing ropes and accessories, light sleeping bags, rucksacks, skis, crampons etcetera for use on land. Fritz had his scuba gear with spare air bottles and he, Ted and I had heavy wet suits.

All this gear was bulky in the extreme; most of it lived in the cabin in kitbags that we crawled over laboriously on the way to the heads. More annoying, however well everything was packed, it always managed to get wet. Though drying clothes was sometimes a problem, they could usually be draped over the engine when it was running, or hung above the stove or the kerosene cabin heater when this was in use (the heater could not really keep pace with the big cabin and generally open door into the cockpit). Nevertheless, *Solo's* thick insulation kept condensation down to a minimum, even in the temperatures that were soon to become normal, of $-1°C$ to $+1°C$. This was a most welcome change after *Ice Bird,* in which the streaming runnels had only dried up when they froze.

But to return to our story. I was asleep in my bunk so did not hear the little party from the port watch singing in the New Year. We must have just crossed the 60th parallel at the time and been entering the Screaming Sixties and the realm of the *Antarctic Pilot,* 'southward of the usual route of vessels'.

I mentioned that our satellite tracking device, *Snow Petrel,* was not intended for current navigation. However, anticipating that we would be in the neighbourhood of the Ballenys in about a week, and that if it were not snowing heavily it would be foggy (the islands only emerge from their

50

clouds for about fifteen days a year), we requested the CSIRO to obtain our position several days ahead by telex from the United States. As it happened, we did make our landfall unaided by the satellite, but it gave our position as less than ten miles from my sextant one. This was a very poor result on my part, but Fritz, who had never expected my navigation to work at all, was impressed. I could not resist sending the rather specious telegram to CSIRO 'Sextant sights confirm accuracy of *Snow Petrel*'.

The really important satellite data that we now began to receive were on the positions and extent of the pack ice. These were obtained by Pieter Arriens, generally using his own set and his Ham designation of VK1PA. Prior arrangements had been made with the Commander of the US Fleet weather facility in Maryland, and at our request forecasts from the US were sent to McMurdo Station in Antarctica, and relayed by Col Christiansen from the Australian base at Davis. The ice reports were based on satellite microwave imagery which is capable of delineating the boundary of pack ice, even through totally cloudy skies. The data were sent to us in the form of a series of latitudes and longitudes that we plotted on our charts. All our experience was to confirm the extraordinary precision of the US forecasts.

What was revealed to us was a development of the earlier situation outlined by the glaciolgist Bill Budd. The Balleny Islands were accessible from the east, a most unusual occurence so early in the season, and open water extended almost to Cape Adare at the entrance of the Ross Sea. Another partially open lead stretched from the Ballenys to Oates Land, but it could be a transitory phenomenon and very likely a trap. West of the Ballenys an enormous area of heavy polar pack extended a good hundred miles north of the group and south in a 150-mile solid sheet to the mainland. It was doubtful if this main polar pack would be breached at all this summer. Westward again, the way was opening towards King George V Land. There would be no time to visit the Ballenys and George V Land too. Choosing the most readily accessible, we laid course for the Ballenys, intending afterwards to visit Cape Adare and, if conditions permitted (a big if), Oates Land. This latter part of Australian territory is, incidentally, the site of a large Russian base, called Leningradskya. They cordially invited us to visit them. We were dubious as to the possibility and, indeed, the partial lead soon closed.

New Year's Day, 1978. Noon found us going fast over a relatively smooth sea under all plain sail. A beautiful chocolate-coloured, light-mantled sooty albatross wheeled past on rigid pinions and twenty or thirty silvery-grey prions or ice birds darted above the pale green sea. The air temperature was + 1°C now, the sea much the same. Peter Donaldson had begun collecting water samples for chemical analysis.

Suddenly we were all startled by a loud menacing rumbling that seemed to emanate from the bowels of the ship. We had no notion what it could be. Our first idea was that the propellor shaft was grinding away. Hasty inspection showed nothing amiss and brought to light the much more startling circumstance that the noise was not coming from anywhere in the ship at all but from *under the water*. We peered over the side anxiously. There could be no possible doubt, the noise was coming up from the sea bed two miles down.

The only conceivable explanation was an underwater eruption or earthquake. We continued sailing south-east, not a little alarmed, while the heavy rumbling vibrations kept on for the next three hours. 'If we see steam bubbling up let us get some hot water for washing up' someone remarked, sounding more light-hearted than any of us felt. Rather to our relief, nothing was seen and the noise ceased as abruptly as it had begun.

The explanation was not forthcoming until after our return to Australia. A *Snow Petrel* position was available for mid-afternoon. This put us in 61°.52'S, 161°.51'E, directly over a transformed fault, according to Dr Quilty of Macquarie University. Moreover, the direction of the fault was north-west to south-east, exactly the way we were steering. There could be no doubt that we had been sailing down the fault line while the mid-ocean plates were in motion, grinding against each other. That being so, Dr Quilty was surprised to find that no Pacific seismograph had monitored the disturbance, which must have been a very small one. Goodness knows what a really big one would have felt like!

The sunset that evening, flaming yellow and pink all across the south-western sky, was continuous with the even more spectacular scarlet and gold sunrise that ran from the south all the way round to east. There was no appreciable darkness. The air temperature had dropped to 0°C and the seawater to -0.4°C. Light flurries of dry powder snow descended from a thickening overcast. Cape pigeons, fulmars and ice birds (prions) swept to and fro across our wake, watched over by a lordly black-browed albatross and his light-mantled sooty opposite number.

I sighted the first ice at 9 am, a tabular berg low down on the southern horizon. As it came nearer the crew gathered in the cockpit to watch, while Ted got out his camera equipment. Only Jack and Fritz were still asleep. Deciding to say nothing to them, we awaited their reactions when they awoke and came on deck. Jack was the first. He relieved himself, never glancing towards the horizon, then stumped down below again. To a call of 'iceberg' he muttered something about that being a likely tale and returned to his bunk. Not a very satisfactory reaction! Fritz was much better. He overheard the word 'iceberg' as he stepped into the cockpit, looked the wrong way and said disgustedly, 'There are no icebergs'. Then glancing over his shoulder, 'Bugger me, there is one!'

Before long icebergs were to be in sight whichever way we looked but we never lost our awe of the waxy monsters. We were to become much closer acquainted with them later when Peter Donaldson began his detailed temperature and salinity measurements in their near vicinity.

By now the sun had become our exclusive steering guide and, while it was only too often hidden by cloud, the twenty-four-hour daylight permitted glimpses of its pale disc now and again. Stamping his feet to keep warm the helmsman steered in much the same fashion as had his Polynesian and Viking predecessors centuries before. The only concession to the present day was the occasional use of Pieter's sun compass, a device reminiscent of a sundial, in which the direction of the shadow, allowing for the sun's roughly 15° per hour progression round the horizon, indicates direction. This was typical of our Oceanic Research Foundation approach, I thought — sail power and sun steering while, at the same time, making full use of such modern developments as satellite ice reports.

Radio contacts had been becoming increasingly unsatisfactory for some time and this was the evening, as it happened, when Jack Pittar found the trouble. A temperature-sensitive component in the radio was playing up. He introduced an electric light bulb into the set to keep it warm. Thereafter it functioned perfectly.

Next day we encountered the pack. The day after, January 4, *Solo* was holed by ice.

This was the occasion for our crucial conference. The leak had been firmly stopped, surplus fuel jettisoned and gear re-stowed to raise the bow and render the site of the damage more accessible, when we gathered together in the cabin. As I had already ascertained, the majority favoured continuing the voyage with more caution and avoiding like the plague being beset in close pack. Of the two who demurred, favouring immediate return to Australia or New Zealand, or even most unrealistically, heading for the Auckland or the Campbell sub-Antarctic islands, one was inexperienced at sea, the other very knowledgeable indeed. It was clear to me that these mistaken councils were emotionally rather than rationally based. The others thought so too and rejected them, but the arguments of the knowledgeable one, even though they were based on rationalisation of his fears, partially undermined several people's confidence during the coming weeks.

The meeting having concluded with a satisfactory consensus, we hoisted the trysail and storm jib and got under way, heading east and north-east along the ice edge, attempting, as the log put it, 'to circle to approach the Ballenys from the east'. Noon on January 5, the close of our third week at sea, found us being forced towards the north-east by close-set streamers of pack, every moment further away from the Ballenys, with the unbroken ice blink to the southward promising no immediate respite.

My diary reflects the depression and tensions of those days.

'Proud of crew's reactions — or most of them. The timid keep re-raising the problems, finding ever new specious reasons for running away. The rest unexpectedly solid ... Too tired for much depression and disappointment. A sound ship would not have been damaged by that impact.' (This estimate proved correct when *Solo* was eventually put on the slip. Three tiny areas, where salt water from the shower had stagnated against a frame, had rusted insidiously beneath the paint. One of these we had struck.) I was no less correct to continue: 'That the impact occurred, however, was my responsibility alone'.

Despite its gloomy ending the third week had put us another 695 miles on our way and within striking distance of our first objective.

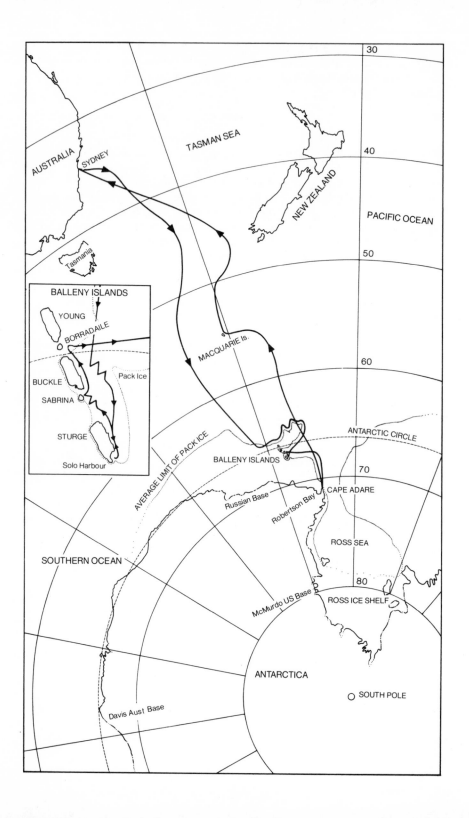

30

AUSTRALIA   SYDNEY   TASMAN SEA   40   NEW ZEALAND   PACIFIC OCEAN

Tasmania   50

BALLENY ISLANDS

YOUNG

BORRADAILE   MACQUARIE Is.   60

BUCKLE   Pack Ice

SABRINA

ANTARCTIC CIRCLE

STURGE

Solo Harbour   BALLENY ISLANDS   70

CAPE ADARE

Russian Base   Robertson Bay

ROSS SEA

SOUTHERN OCEAN   80

McMurdo US Base   ROSS ICE SHELF

ANTARCTICA

○ SOUTH POLE

Davis Aust Base

Chapter 4

Untrodden Snows
Sturge Island

T he next two days were among the most frustrating of the voyage. Every time we attempted to turn southwards the pack forced us back north again. This was not over good for morale but I was glad to see how positively the crew were behaving. Ted Rayment seriously got down to the demanding task of working out film sequences, though his visits to inspect the patch remained very frequent — despite efforts by Lars and myself to reassure him. Fritz was not well again and Peter Donaldson had developed swelling of the feet at the site of an old frostbite. This responded very satisfactorily to the drug Ronicol. Exercise for the feet, while desirable, was impracticable in the confined space aboard.

'How long will the morale of the crew hold out against impatience?' I wrote.

Everything comes to an end and on the afternoon of January 7 we cautiously angled southward, and south-westward the following day. The sea was still dotted with ice floes in various stages of disintegration, with more dangerous growlers (of which more later) and bergs, which were relatively easily seen. A moment's carelessness when I was at the helm could well have had serious consequences, though I think less serious than Peter Donaldson imagined. Still, in fairness, I will quote his account verbatim.

> Lars went for a pee and, glancing up, saw a bergy-bit the size of a house appear out of the mist like a phantom, dead ahead and only a few boat-lengths distant. David was steering away quite unconcerned. 'What are you going to do about that lump of ice?' Lars asked in his usual deadpan manner. 'What lump of ice?' asked David. 'That bloody iceberg.' There was a pause, 'S . . .' and David frantically spun the helm.

'Fog, brief gale, mist', the log records the monotonous sequence. But only light pack was encountered and *Solo* drove on into the west, as if 'in a wide still corridor like an enormous lead protected by the distant arms of the pack', over an 'opalescent sea . . . the wide horizon dotted with blue bergs'. Pack thickened and, at 1 am on January 9 we hove-to in a vast polynia (a 'lake' of open water in the midst of the pack) until such time as a glimpse of the sun should tell us our direction. An unreal world, it seemed. A minke whale broke surface; a skua gull flew by. Then all was still again. Ted and Peter Donaldson brought out their equipment and, leaning on the rail, I outlined for the camera our progress so far and our hopes for the future.

Meanwhile Jack Pittar had been working with the batteries for a solid eight hours until he was satisfied that their charging rate was adequate. Not satisfied with this *tour de force* he then set about checking over the Dick Smith walkie-talkies in anticipation of a landing.

The sun peeped through and we got under way. Eight am and Peter Donaldson, who was in the rigging conning *Solo* through the leads, shouted 'LAND!' — Young and Buckle Islands in the Ballenys, away to the south-west. Excitement ran high. As the hours went by we zig-zagged through the pack, guided by glimpses of the sun, for the land was soon hidden by falling snow. The Antarctic Circle was crossed about noon.

It was in 1839 that the sealing captain Balleny of the schooner *Eliza Scott,* with the cutter *Sabrina* in company, first sighted the islands named after him. From the log of *Eliza Scott* February 9.

At 11 am noticed a darkish appearance to the S.W.: observed the latitude to be 66°.37′S by mer. alt. : wind north. At noon the sun shone brightly: saw the appearance of land to the S.W. extending from west to about south — ran for it: at 4 h made it out distinctly to be land. At 8 h pm (having run S.W. 22 m) got within 5 miles of it, when we saw another piece of land of great height, bearing W. by S. At sunset we distinctly made them out to be three separate islands of good size, but the western one the longest. Lay-to all night off the middle island.

Smoke was seen issuing from two craters on the middle island (Buckle Island). None was seen by Ross when he sighted the Ballenys five years later, but when Borchgrevink passed the islands in 1899 Buckle was again smoking. No activity has been observed since 1904.

The Balleny chain of three large and two smaller islands is about a hundred miles long and straddles the Antarctic circle about 160 miles north of the mainland. From north-west to south-east are Young Island, Borradaile, Buckle, Sabrina and Sturge, the last of which is also the largest being twenty miles long. All are named after the 'spirited merchants who united with Mr Enderby in sending out this expedition'. All are volcanic and thickly covered with ice, which descends to the sea at every break in the cliffs, forming tongues which project a mile or more seaward. The summits are undulating and snow-covered but are guarded by precipices between 300 and 700 metres high, for the most part topped by menacing hanging glaciers. Prior to our visit there had been five seaborne landings in the group and half a dozen (in 1959, 1964 and 1965) by helicopters from icebreakers. Most landings were made only with great difficulty and had been fleeting in the extreme. All early reports agree that the neighbourhood of the Ballenys abounded in whales, a circumstance that attracted whaling expeditions from the Soviet Union and Norway (a commentary on their efficiency was the tiny handful of whales that we sighted).

A tragic incident occurred on Christmas Day 1928. A Gypsy Moth plane took off from the whaling factory ship *Kosmos* in clear weather to fly to the

Ballenys. It was never seen again. We were requested by the Norwegian Embassy to keep an eye out for the wreckage but saw no sign of it.

Despite the thickening weather we closed the Ballenys with great hopes. Very different, apparently, had been the effect of sighting the islands upon Bernacchi, Borchgrevink's second-in command. In 1899 he wrote:

> One sight in bad weather of that sinister coast is enough to make a landsman dream for weeks of shipwrecks, perils and death. I can imagine no greater punishment than to be 'left alone to live forgotten and die forlorn' on that desolate shore.

The land continued to elude us though a sun sight at 1 pm put us opposite the northern tip of Buckle Island. As we headed diagonally in towards the southern end of the island the easterly breeze rapidly increased in strength and the glass began to fall steeply. Fog compounded the falling snow and reduced visibility still further. All the signs suggested that an easterly gale was imminent. We were in an unenviable position.

The Ballenys are perched on the very junction of two turbulent and opposing weather and current systems. To the north, the westerlies of the 'Screaming Sixties' howl round the world, driving the sea surface before them in the form of the West Wind Drift. To the south, the polar easterly winds and corresponding west-going current prevail. The actual meeting place of these air and water masses is variable and stormy in the extreme, so that the Ballenys experience westerlies and easterlies in quick succession, generally accompanied by heavy precipitation.

By early afternoon on January 9 the wind had strengthened to a strong easterly gale of force 9. The unseen Buckle Island made a dangerous lee shore, complicated by the fact that, while the main polar pack was beyond the island to the west, there was not a little east of it as well. This pack could be expected to drive eastwards before the gale, putting *Solo* at risk of being trapped between the ice and the cliffs of the land. Coming at last to an extensive polynia, whose boundaries were lost in the mist, we hove-to under the trysail. This was not a success as the yacht fore-reached (forged ahead) so fast that she was continually coming up against the limits of her prison. It was Lars and Peter who spotted from the rigging the small lead that enabled us to motor out to the eastward clear of the pack ice and into open water. As Peter wrote:

> David said his usual 'Let's suck it and see' and we hove-to. Soon a five or six metre heavy swell developed and great chunks of heaving grinding pack-ice started closing in. Lars and I put goggles on and climbed about half way up the sixty foot mast. One second the boat would roll sending the mast arcing over us and slackening the stays, then it would yaw back and the tightened stays would try to catapult us into the boiling sea. Although standing next to each other, we had to shout to be heard above the deafening scream of the wind in the rigging. Through the driving spray we spotted a small lead in the pack-ice . . . I fell into bed exhausted whilst Lars and Pieter negotiated more pack-ice and hove-to again in more open water.

By then the wind had eased considerably. *Solo* lay most conveniently a-hull (that is, without any sail at all), when she drifted very little faster than the wind-driven ice floes. Every now and then we had to unlash the helm and steer clear of some uncooperative mass of ice that was surging up and down among the rollers, using either the storm jib or the motor to give us steerage way. All through January 10 we lay offshore in this fashion, while Lars worked on a slipping clutch and Jack toiled unavailingly at the radar. Twice unidentifiable land loomed up through the mist to leeward. Then, at 11 pm, a conical stack named Scott Cone, off the southern end of Buckle Island and some three miles off, appeared between snow showers and happily confirmed our dead reckoning. We were all very anxious to attempt a landing, of course, but the surf kicked up by the gale was liable to hamper us even after the weather had cleared. Meanwhile, the crew set to to prepare landing (mostly mountaineering) equipment and rations. Jack announced that he was working on the design of a great catapult to shoot Fritz ashore, and sure enough I dreamed that night of the catapulted Fritz scuttling, crampons and all, up a vertical ice face.

January 11 saw some temporary improvement, then the glass, which had been rising, plummetted to a new frightening low of 950 mb (the normal for the Ballenys at that time of year was 990 mb). The wind veered into the north and increased to near hurricane strength — force 11. Despite the strength of the storm with its seventy-knot gusts, we were able to continue comfortably a-hull, with Dot carrying on with her cooking, for the pack to windward effectively blanketed the seas. The only casualty was a cut on the nose that I sustained from a piece of ice falling from the rigging.

The northerly storm continued to blow for twenty-seven hours all told and did not abate until the early hours of Friday January 13. This was to prove a particularly auspicious day for us. The twenty-mile-long Sturge Island, the largest and southernmost of the Ballenys, was impenetrably locked in the pack at the time of the most recent satellite ice report, the ice edge being a full twenty miles north of Sturge, between it and Buckle. Now at 2 am the storm clouds rolled away like drawn curtains revealing the mighty rock and ice bastions of Sturge Island some twenty miles to the southward across an ice-free sea. The northerly storm had driven the ice before it and cleared a path for us. Here was a heaven-sent opportunity. We made sail immediately and started the motor for good measure.

No landing on Sturge Island had ever been made from the sea. On the morning of January 31, 1965, a joint US-New Zealand party from the icebreaker *USS Glacier* was flown by helicopter to the island and with difficulty found an ice-free site where 'a touch landing lasting perhaps ten seconds was made during which time Malcolm Ford jumped out and gathered up a handful of rocks'. In the evening of the same day two further helicopter landings were made. These were significant in overlooking 'probably the only relatively safe boat landing place on the island'. This estimate by Barry Waterhouse, leader of the *Glacier* expedition, we were shortly able to confirm. His landings, of which we were unaware at the time, are worth describing in his own words.

Two landings by harness and winch were made by the writer, on rock outcrops near the south-eastern extremity of the Island, near the end of a prominent ice tongue east of Cape Smyth; and although these outcrops might be considered islets, they were, at the time, land-tied by an ice-capped shingle spit. During this exercise the helicopter remained airborne, largely as a precautionary measure against sudden snow showers which were encountered at frequent intervals. Nevertheless, even though movement on the rock was restricted, the writer collected good sample of in situ rock for a radius of about 15 ft from the helicopter.

By 8.45 am *Solo* had come up with the land. The beetling cliffs of Cape Freeman (named after Balleny's ill-fated lieutenant) towered 400 metres up into swirling mists, which parted ever and anon to reveal the undulating ice cap of the island 700 metres above. Twenty-metre icicles festooned the buttresses and everywhere seabirds wheeled. On every ledge petrels were nesting. We closed the land to three cables (three hundred metres) off and turned south along the eastern shore, anxiously watching the echo sounder, which read six fathoms for the most part, for the sudden rise denoting uncharted underwater pinnacles. The numerous grounded bergs in our path indicated the presence of shoals and reefs and mist patches and snow showers suggested caution. Ted Rayment was filming. He wrote:

> It did however have a rugged grandeur and awesome beauty about it and I was so enthralled filming that I temporarily forgot how cold my hands were getting. My biggest problem filming on deck was keeping my hands warm. I could not operate with my heavy mittens on and had to resort to light woollen gloves so I could feel the lens, but these offered no protection from the wind, and with the wind-chill factor at times dropping the temperature down to about minus twenty this was rather restricting! Peter had the same problem operating the Stellavox.

The red, yellow and brown volcanic tuffs and basalts of Cape Freeman gradually gave way to steep undercut snow slopes and then to ten miles of ice piedmont (shelf), fed by valley glaciers spilling over from the summit ice cap and fronted by ice cliffs forty to sixty metres high. We soon moved further out from the base of the ice cliffs, both to avoid the brash and pack ice at their foot and to be well clear should a berg decide to calve from their crevassed faces. The strata in the ice could be clearly seen, each winter's compacted snowfall being delineated by wind blown dust from the soft volcanic rock deposited in summer.

'It is like the growth rings of trees' explained Fritz, who had been reading up on the Antarctic. 'You can find radioactivity in the layers deposited since Hiroshima. Earlier than that you find the dust that was blown round the world when the volcano Krakatoa blew up in the eighteen eighty somethings. When you bore down thousands of feet into the ice you can bring up samples that were fresh water 10 000 years ago.' We were all a trifle awed. Sturge Island was a microcosm of the Antarctic, where the main types of rock and ice structure could be seen more or less at a glance.

It is worth making a few general points here about the Antarctic, for there is much confusion about it. Despite its formidable ice cap, the continent is, of course, real land — rock mostly, with a little rudimentary soil on its fringes. Apart from some coastal areas and certain strangely ice-free 'dry valleys', that together make up ten per cent of the surface and support mosses and lichens, the remaining ninety per cent is covered by a sheet of ice up to 4.5 kilometres thick, that is pierced here and there and rimmed by vast mountains. The ice is plastic; between the ranges it moves slowly over the down slope ultimately to reach the sea in great ice sheets and glaciers.

The land was not always icebound. Up to between fifty and sixty million years ago it was joined to Australia and, earlier still, to South Africa and India as well. Fossils of reptiles that crawled through Antarctica's one-time tropical swamps have been discovered; coal measures bear mute witness to a period when the continent was for a very long time afforested.

Although the annual rainfall equivalent at the South Pole is only a tenth of that at Alice Springs in Central Australia, with temperatures rarely reaching zero and figures as low as $-88°C$ having been recorded, it does not melt appreciably; it accumulates and becomes consolidated into ice and this ice moves seawards. At the coast the continental ice pushes far out to sea in enormous floating ice shelves up to 750 metres thick and hundreds of kilometres long (the Ross Ice Shelf is larger than France).

The last act of the drama begins when the terminal margins of the ice shelves and glacier tongues 'calve' to form icebergs, enormous flat-topped tabular bergs in the case of the shelves and more rounded denser bergs from the glaciers. Anything from two thirds to seven eighths of the iceberg will be under water depending on the density of the ice composing it. Generally it will tower fifty metres or so up into the air; some monsters are 100 kilometres and more long. When the sea freezes over in winter the bergs are trapped. Then the spring thaw releases them and they drift northwards in the short summer before again being trapped. But steadily, season by season, they move further out from the coast. Some run aground on shoals, weather away and break up there. This process may be protracted. An iceberg that I saw aground off the South Orkneys in 1974 was still eight kilometres long; seven years earlier it had been twice that size.

Most bergs escape shipwreck, however, and the time must come when they finally break free of the pack. From then on, floating northward through ever warmer water and buffeted by storm waves, their days are numbered. The last stage is usually a growler, a rounded lump of very dense ice from the core of the iceberg, that wallows awash with a hollow roaring sound. Growlers are difficult to spot and a great menace to shipping. It was Fritz out of all the crew who came to worry about them most. His 'formula' was to become familiar when he called me to come on watch. 'It is pretty shitty outside and there are a lot of GRROWLERS.'

The feasibility of towing icebergs to Australia as a source of fresh water for arid regions is under active investigation. Later in the voyage Peter Donaldson was to make detailed measurements of temperature and salinity in the vicinity of bergs as part of this study.

Pack ice, in contrast to icebergs, originates from the freezing of the sea's surface — salt water. Something like a metre freezes each winter so, with successive accretions and rafting, floes are usually several times this thickness. In summer the relatively unbroken ice sheet breaks up into separate floes that may be jammed together or separated by leads. An unexpected quality of pack ice can be of great service to seamen. Despite its being frozen sea water, the salt progressively leaches out of the floes until, after a year or at most two, the ice becomes fresh and can be melted and drunk.

Vast rock buttresses, glaciers, ice shelves, bergs and pack ice passed before us in grand array as we motored down the coast of Sturge Island. What was the attraction of this bleak land, I asked myself? Over and above

Cartoon by Ted Rayment

scientific curiosity it draws back again and again those who once have known its spell. Why? I suspect something adventurous in the human spirit responds to the very starkness of its challenge — like those old Vikings in Kipling's poem, *Harp Song of the Dane Women*.

What is a woman that you forsake her,
And the hearth-fire and the home-acre,
To go with the old grey widow-maker?

She has no house to lay a guest in —
But one chill bed for all to rest in,
That the pale suns and the stray bergs nest in.

The unrolling panorama of Sturge Island was magnificent but my musings brought us no nearer a possible landing space. Not until Cape Smyth, twenty miles down the coast at the south-east corner, hove in sight did any sign of a break appear in that daunting wall. A rocky ice-capped hill, off the cape and about 100 metres high, that at first appeared to be an islet, was seen as we approached to be connected to a snow slope under Cape Smyth by a substantial snow-covered shingle spit perhaps half a kilometre long. Being ignorant of Barry Waterhouse's helicopter landing, the sight of the shingle spit threw us all into a state of highest excitement. Against its northern side massive ice floes were grinding in the swell left over from the northerly storm we had so lately experienced. But what of the southern side? Might it not provide a sheltered landing place?

The little peninsula was soon seen to extend out in an east-south-easterly direction. In line with it and its rocky termination were four off-lying rock stacks rising vertically out of the sea. We felt our way between them, watching the echo sounder very carefully. Yes, there *was* a comparatively sheltered lee to the shingle spit, albeit fronted by some large floes and cut off from us by a line of close small pack. With Lars aloft in the rigging and

61

the engine dead slow we nudged the line of small pack ice. Almost imperceptibly the floes moved aside from *Solo's* bow, as I shoved the gear lever in and out of neutral. Lars called down an occasional 'starboard' or 'port' and Ted's camera whirred. Ten minutes and we were through, motoring up towards the spit. At 2.45 pm that January 13 in seven fathoms (fourteen metres) the anchor was let go for the first time since leaving Sydney. According to a subsequent satellite fix from *Snow Petrel* the position was 67°.34′S, 164°.52′E. We lay placidly two cables offshore, the very first ship to find a haven anywhere in the Ballenys. We applied to name the place 'Solo Harbour', a request that was subsequently granted.

Shore-going equipment — spare clothing, ice axes, ropes, collecting bags, geological hammers, walkie-talkies, cameras and rations — had long been ready and the landing parties selected. Lars and I would look after the ship. This was no light responsibility; our harbour was protected from the north and west and partly from the east but it was entirely open to the south where the main polar pack was hovering just below the horizon, its menacing presence revealed by ice blink. A southerly wind would bring back that pack, which might well remain until the following summer (this, in fact, it did). Any ship caught in the harbour would be crushed flat by the heaped up floes piling up against the shingle spit. Lars and I, therefore, kept a vigilant weather eye out.

The Beaufort surf boat was inflated and launched over the side and the 25 hp Evinrude brought up from below and mounted. Both shore party and the *Solo* anchor watch would keep their walkie-talkies switched on at all times. The amazing Evinrude started at the second pull and we were off. There was reason to bless the propellor guard for the harbour was thickly strewn with brash ice. Closer in, it became apparent that the surge was heavy, the worn floes alternately sweeping up to the spit and sucking back with the undertow. After a tour of inspection I picked the most likely spot and nosed in between the surging floes. They were backed by half a metre of uncovered shingle topped by a three-metre vertical wall of snow. I was landing Ted, Fritz, Peter Donaldson and Pieter Arriens.

A wave swept us up to the shingle. With an almighty leap Pieter was out, unfortunately without the painter. Since he had no ice axe either, the unfortunate explorer was unable to climb up the snow wall and remained for the next ten minutes pressed against it, watched with some interest by a half-grown Weddell seal that weaved to and fro in the water at his feet, and encouraged by our helpful shouts of 'See you next year'. Then we brought up against a grounded floe, Fritz secured the painter to an ice axe and in a moment the rest were scrambling ashore and passing up their gear.

Returning to *Solo,* I collected Dot and Jack and started for the spit again. Ted, who was smug about keeping his feet dry, was ready to film the occasion. Jack made it successfully but Dot for some reason missed the grounded floe and jumped out onto a tiny floating one. There was barely room for her to crouch down on hands and knees as it gyrated back and forth in the swell. Dot herself wrote in her diary.

> I had a certain amount of trouble landing. Had to jump on to a small ice floe which began to surge out to sea again with me aboard ... Jump, they all said, but I wanted to wait until the wave came back in. However under their insistence I did jump into quite deep water so that I was wet

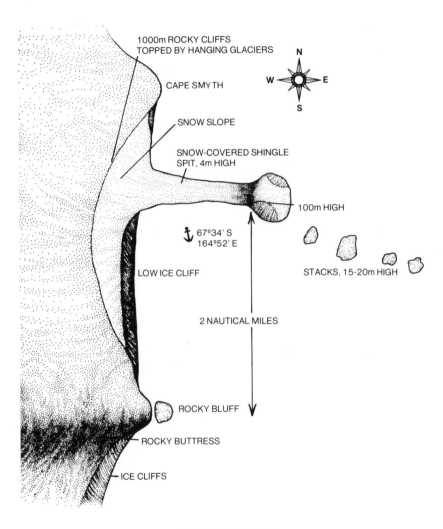

1000m ROCKY CLIFFS
TOPPED BY HANGING GLACIERS

CAPE SMYTH

SNOW SLOPE

SNOW-COVERED SHINGLE
SPIT, 4m HIGH

100m HIGH

⚓ 67°34' S
164°52' E

LOW ICE CLIFF

STACKS, 15-20m HIGH

2 NAUTICAL MILES

ROCKY BLUFF

ROCKY BUTTRESS

ICE CLIFFS

SOLO HARBOUR

and my camera full. What a laugh. All on film with my reactions and antics. (Ted Rayment made amends for his ungallant pictures by dismantling and drying Dot's camera.)

I had stood by in the Beaufort while all this was going on, not a little concerned that Dot might have to be rescued from the sub-zero water. The walkie-talkie in the Beaufort came alive.

'Rubber Duck from *Solo*. Are you having fun?'

'*Solo* from Rubber Duck. All ashore, some wet feet.'

'Shore party from Rubber Duck, how are things going?'

'Rubber Duck from shore party. Pieter collecting rocks.'

'Can you pick him up later to take him to the rocky bluff you agreed on? Peter is getting a sound track of Weddell seal noises and picking up seaweed. Fritz and Dot are talking to the seals — there seem to be about twelve. No penguins but several fulmars and skuas.'

'Romeo, Ted. Will pick up Pieter with the rest of you about six. Rubber Duck, out.'

Feeling deeply content I rejoined Lars aboard. The rum bottle came out, for we believed we had earned a celebration. 'Skol!' We amused ourselves watching the activities of the shore party through the binoculars, but never neglected to glance towards the ice blink to southward, nor to keep testing the direction of the wind. Reassured, we lowered the grab and winched up a bottom sample of ooze.

Of the Weddell seals Dot wrote.

> I was able to play with one's tail or flippers and really it hardly reacted. Lovely brown eyes with pink round the edges. They have lovely fine silky coats sometimes brown with grey but often a spotted sort of yellow and grey. Three skuas were fighting over the remains of a snow petrel and were very curious, allowing us to get quite close. Lots of cape pigeons and fulmars about. Did some filming, rock gathering, etc., until 6 pm when we returned to *Solo,* all in one trip this time.

The excellent performance of the Beaufort had convinced me that she could carry the whole seven of us safely in one go. Hanging on with difficulty to the grounded floe, I called on everyone to embark. 'Shouldn't we make two trips, skipper?' Fritz asked. 'FRITZ!' I roared, in no mood to hold the lively boat longer than necessary. He hastily slithered aboard. This time we had managed it dry shod.

The others having been deposited aboard *Solo,* Pieter with his specimen sacks and geological hammers and I roared off down the harbour, skipping gaily over brash ice with a confidence born of inexperience, to the black rocky bluff some two miles away on the main island, that Pieter had previously earmarked. The surge was much greater here; the ice-polished black rocks shiny and uninviting. I stepped onto a ledge, holding the painter; Pieter tossed out his gear and clambered hastily out of reach of the swells. I jumped back in and pushed off.

Facing page • *left* **Monolith on Sabrina Island**   *top right* **Monolith from *Solo***   *centre & bottom right* **Adélie rookery on Sabrina Island**

Following pages • *top* **Peter Donaldson and Jack Pittar work on the boat in Solo Harbour**   *bottom* **Peter Donaldson making salinity tests**   **Salinity testing takes *Solo* closer to an iceberg**

The rocks that fringe the polar tidelines are unique in their stark polished cleanness for the ice that scrapes against them ensures that no barnacle, sea anemone or limpet should take hold. This extreme barrenness is deceptive, however, for only two or three metres beneath the surface, below the level of the floes, the Antarctic seabed is a veritable garden of seaweeds, spider crabs, sea urchins and sluggish bottom dwelling fish, whose blood contains glyco-protein anti-freeze compounds. I was not surprised, therefore, to spot some singularly beautiful pink and blue jellyfish near Pieter's rock. I had no net with me so, in the cause of science, but reluctantly for the sea temperature was − 1.4°C., I fished for them by hand. When two good specimens reposed safely in plastic bags honour was satisfied and I started the motor. Pieter was to be picked up later.

The engine revved well enough but, when I put it in gear, nothing happened. A quick inspection showed that the sheer pin, that is constructed to break in place of the propellor, had indeed fractured during my rather intemperate dash through the brash ice shortly before. It is no big thing to replace a sheer pin but, to my chagrin, I found that I had carelessly left behind on *Solo* the spare pin and the pliers to fit it that should have been aboard Rubber Duck. There was nothing for it but to strip off my parka, squat in the bow and start paddling the two miles back to *Solo*. This took me an hour.

It was particularly pleasing that Pieter was obtaining oriented rock samples, that have to be carefully chipped out of the living rock, to enable studies to be made of the earth's past magnetic fields and hence something of its geological history. No such specimens had ever been obtained from the Ballenys before. Dr Larry Embleton of the CSIRO North Ryde and Dr Pat Quilty of Macquarie University were to study Pieter's Sturge Island rocks. Their crystalline structure is remarkably beautiful.

Shortly after I had regained *Solo* and retired below to a well-earned rest a new drama occurred. Peter Donaldson spotted a snow petrel in the water in obvious difficulties, awash, with only its head and one wing showing. Jumping into the Beaufort, he brought it aboard. There was no sign of injury so he carefully wrapped it in a towel and nursed the beautiful snow-white creature. Let Dot take up the tale:

> Peter nursed it in a towel for ages, then in my red pack with (chemical) hand warmers. Just as I got to bed about 4.10 am it got out of the bag, trotted round the cabin and onto Lars' bunk. I was hoping he would wake to find a 'bird' in his bunk, something he was always wishing for!

Snow petrels are as graceful as fluttering snow flakes in flight but their feet are oversized and floppy so that when walking on any surface other than smooth snow they are liable to trip over their feet and overbalance. This one was no exception. After a few stumbles it took up station on the crockery rack, preened its feathers for a while, then tucked its head under its wing and went to sleep till morning. Peter hoped − if the bird were dry enough − to release it some time that day.

About 9 pm Lars, Jack and Ted went off in the Beaufort to pick up Pieter off his rock with his by then substantial sack of samples. The swell had increased and at one time the bow of Rubber Duck was stranded high on

Facing page • *top* **Approaching Cape Adare** *bottom* **Admiralty Range behind Cape Adare − Mount Minto, the highest peak, is clearly visible**

the rock while the stern with its vulnerable outboard was awash two metres below it, while all hands struggled frantically to prevent a capsize or a swamping. It was a near thing, but they got off safely, though all somewhat shaken by the experience. That night we celebrated with two bottles of champagne that Pieter opportunely produced, Dot's rum and chocolate mixture and a Chinese-type meal of canned tuna, rice and assorted vegetables.

Apart from the anchor watch, the ship's company slept late next morning. Pieter prepared the winch for more bottom specimens, while his namesake, the other Peter, spent a busy two hours sealing and labelling biological specimens (including my jelly fish) in plastic bags, breaking off now and again to see to the still drowsy snow petrel. There was no wind and mist wreaths gently drifted across the anchorage. The barometer was steady at the regional normal of 990.8 mb; the weather seemed settled.

At 10 am an unwelcome southerly breeze began to stir and within minutes had set in steady and was strengthening. This was what I had been dreading. Already there were some big new floes in the anchorage and long streamers of pack had appeared outside during the night. An ominous white line pencilled the southern horizon under the ice blink. The main pack was less than three miles off (the distance to the sea horizon) and bearing down upon us.

'Let us get going' I said.

'I would like just five minutes on the gravel spit to collect more specimens' announced Pieter.

'But you had hours there yesterday and anyway you said loose stones were not much use.'

'It is very important that I get the specimens'.

'Are you really sure that five minutes will do — *literally?*'

'Well, half an hour perhaps.'

I hesitated. The pack was still a long way off but ice conditions can change with bewildering rapidity and the stakes for misjudgment were far too high.

'Lars?'

'If it was me I would go now.'

'OK, everyone on deck. Will you start the motor, Jack, and the anchor windlass. Lars, how about Rubber Duck and the outboard.' Pieter began to argue. Lars turned to him with an unconscious paraphrase of Captain Freeman of Balleny's *Sabrina,* who 'jumped out and got a few stones, but was up to his middle in water'. (February 12, 1839, on Borradaile, the first recorded landing south of the Antarctic Circle.)

'I would not risk the ship for a few stones' Lars said.

'I resent that description of valuable scientific specimens' replied Pieter heatedly, but we were all too busy getting under way to listen to him.

Two of the first Adélie penguins we had seen at Sturge Island peered at us from a small floe. Ted was hard put to it to film the occasion. He explains his difficulty of reacting at short notice.

As I struggled into my clothes I was again made aware of just how difficult it was to capture on film any emergency. Dressing oneself into twenty items of clothing took nearly fifteen minutes — sometimes even longer in very rough weather. Then I had to get the camera out of its locker forward and rush back to take the battery off its charger in a locker down aft, meanwhile falling over Peter who was doing the same thing with the sound gear. This almost comical and rather ungainly event took place more times than I can remember and I cursed the many times I had missed a good sequence because of it. Yet there was no alternative. In a boat of *Solo's* size nothing could just be put down without the risk of its being flung from one side of the ship to the other.

This time, since the belt on the hydraulic windlass was slipping, Ted was in good time to film our departure. It was 10.30 am when the dripping anchor came aboard and we threaded our way out between the perceptibly thickening pack and the rock stacks off Cape Smyth. *Solo* had lain for twenty hours in the bay, the first ship, as far as we know, to anchor anywhere in the Balleny group.

Since there was no way open to the south and west we retraced our course up the east coast of Sturge Island, our objective Sabrina Islet, which lay a few miles south of the middle big island, Buckle, and sixty miles north from Cape Smyth. Pieter, his ill humour forgotten, made a stout performance of bottom dredging, filmed by Ted. The main contents of the grab was ooze, composed of the microscopic skeletons of foraminifera, but there was at least one interesting-looking worm as well.

By now Peter's snow petrel had woken up and appeared increasingly restless so its protector decided it was time to let it go. Ted got out his camera again, with Fritz doing the sound recording this time. I noticed with amusement that Ted had labelled the sequence 'Interview with Bird'.

The snowy white creature showed signs of excitement when Peter brought it into the cockpit, stretching its neck and arching its wings. But could it manage the take-off and then stay aloft? All of us were concerned. There was nothing for it but to put the matter to the test. Peter lifted the petrel high in the air, its wings began to beat and it flapped away from his hand. At first the flight path dipped dangerously near the water and we held our breaths. Would it make it? Then the wing beats strengthened and the petrel soared, rapidly diminishing in the distance. The delighted expression on Peter's face was a picture.

As the afternoon wore on it became clear that we were outdistancing the northward-moving pack. Dot made a hundred pikelets for tea at six. They were immediately consumed by us clustering gallahs. We took departure from Cape Freeman, the northern tip of Sturge Island, at 8 pm and shaped our course northward by the sun setting between layers of stratus cloud. At 11 pm a sight of Buckle Island confirmed we were on the correct bearing.

The last few days' freedom from pack ice was not to last. Half way to Buckle and Sabrina islands extensive but broken fields were encountered drifting in from the west and *Solo* had to zig-zag from lead to lead, conned by a man from aloft. Sabrina Island with its unmistakeable monolith came into view by the light of the cloud-obscured midnight sun soon after 1 am on January 15. To and fro we wound our way, now under power, now under sail as the wind served. It was about eight o'clock when *Solo* came up with the same Scott Pillar that we had last seen through the fog four days before and it could be seen that the way to Sabrina lay open.

Chapter 5

The Lonely Monolith
Sabrina Islet

W hy Sabrina should be denied the dignity of 'island' and labelled 'islet' by the *Admiralty Pilot* I do not know, for its terrain is substantial and varied and its broad sloping summit is 150 metres or so above the sea. The 'most remarkable feature', again according to the *Pilot*, 'is a sharp pinnacle rock, broad at the base, tapering to a point and about 78 metres high'. This monolith rises towards the southern end of the islet and between it and the main mass stretches a snow-covered shingle spit, not unlike that bounding Solo Harbour at Sturge Island. We were to find that its configuration had altered considerably since the last expedition to Sabrina in 1965.

All the landings on Sabrina had been made on the shingle spit, the first being by a French party from the *Commandant Charcot* in 1949. In 1965 a helicopter survey party from *USS Glacier* camped on a saddle above the spit, where 100 knot winds kept them marooned for three days. Despite the relatively large number of our predecessors (four landings, three of them by helicopter) we had little doubt that much remained to be discovered — and so it proved, especially when Peter's lichen specimens came to be examined by Antarctic Division biologists. Furthermore, as we skirted the rocky slopes, stained green and red with penguin droppings and lichens and studded with ninepin-like rows of penguins, I spotted a second likely landing place at the foot of a boulder slope on the virgin north shore.

The breeze was light and from the west and the sheltered eastern side of the shingle spit was free of floes, though there was a good deal of pack in the vicinity. This last consideration constrained us to lower sail and heave-to a-hull for the sake of greater mobility rather than come to anchor when we arrived off the spit at 10 am, January 5. The first landing party got ready, with Lars, Fritz and myself to remain as anchor watch.

We were not the first yacht to visit the Ballenys, I reflected, as the shore party made their preparations. Balleny's original little flotilla had comprised the schooner *Eliza Scott* and the cutter *Sabrina* under Captain Freeman (he who made the first landing south of the Antarctic Circle and in the Ballenys). Now the sealing firm of Enderby, who were notable patrons of Antarctic exploration, sometimes bought up old racing yachts which had become outdated for the regattas at Cowes, and fitted them out for Antarctic service. One such was *Sabrina*. She was a cutter of fifty-four tons, which compares with *Solo's* thirty-five, allowing for the contrast in design whereby *Sabrina* was of far heavier displacement. No illustration of *Sabrina* survives, but she must have differed very little in her lines from the larger sixty-five ton cutter *Beaufoy,* that sailed in company with Captain James Weddell's brig *Jane* (he was another of Enderby's skippers) to the extraordinary latitude of 74°.15′S in 1823.

Sad to say, neither Captain Freeman and his gallant crew, nor his hard-won stones from Borradaile Island, nor *Sabrina* herself ever saw England again. On March 24, 1839, somewhere near 52°S, 94°E, one of the stormiest parts of the Southern Ocean, the staunch little cutter was overwhelmed in a fearful storm and lost with all hands. I was determined, if it rested within my power, that *Solo* should not fare likewise.

By now Rubber Duck was in the water, with spare shear pins, tools, pumps, paddles, repair kit and walkie-talkies. Ted and Peter prudently wrapped their cameras and sound recording equipment in layers of plastic. Pieter Arriens was well equipped with two geological hammers, sacks for specimens and cameras. The other Peter had his collecting bags and bottles. Spare clothing and emergency iron rations were added. An appreciable surf was breaking on the steep shingle bank when Lars pushed off with the Peters and Ted and cautiously closed the islet, while I brought *Solo* in as close as I dared in support. Lars timed the waves to a nicety and got everybody ashore more or less dry shod. He returned to *Solo* and did the same for Dot and Jack.

The landing party were entranced. For several it was their first experience of the 'Little People' en masse and one's first experience of an Adélie penguin rookery is quite unforgettable. The main rookery was on a saddle 100 metres above the sea. It was reached up a steep snow slope, up and down which lines of penguins were solemnly picking their way. Those going up had their backs to the explorers and were black. The descending column to their right presented their white waistcoats to the observers. Heads bent forward on their chests, they picked their way with meticulous care and never missed a step. On level ground (snow covered) some wandered about over the snow among the somnolent forms of Weddell seals while the more enterprising picked their way delicately across the close-packed floes to the westward on their way to capture fish and krill suppers for their mates and chicks waiting on the saddle.

Dot was enthralled. She started playing with a seal which opened its mouth and grumbled then, like all seals when disturbed, burst into tears — or rather its great brown eyes, so perfectly adapted to underwater vision half a kilometre down, filled with moisture to help it focus on the intruder. Pieter Arriens set to work breaking off oriented rock samples from the base of the Monolith. He was able to reach it on foot because it was now joined to the main mass of Sabrina Islet by the shingle spit. This had not been the case when the *Pilot Book* was written, nor even during the last visit to Sabrina in 1965. Both the descriptions and a very clear photograph make it clear that the spit had then terminated well short of the Monolith.

Ted set up his camera on a tripod and was soon busy filming the Adélie penguins. The tripod was in case they would not let him come close enough to use a hand-held camera, but he need not have worried. Once he glanced down to find a small figure peering up at the camera from within the legs of the tripod. At the sight of Ted's face it uttered a startled 'Ark Ark' and waddled hastily off.

Leaving Pieter to his labours and abandoning the tripod, the rest of the party climbed up the 100-metre snow and ice-covered scree slope to the rookery. 'I rather wish I'd had a smell filter' Ted wrote, 'as the odour from guano and stale urine is pretty strong.' But I have found from experience that the nose very soon becomes anaesthetised against the smell of a rookery. As for Peter Donaldson, his description is almost lyrical.

Some shyly kept their distance from us whilst others would march boldly up to us, fix one with a baleful wise eye and say 'Arrk'. In the rookeries we were greeted by a cacaphony of raucous calling as adults guarded their chicks. Some rascals used the diversion of our presence to steal stones from their neighbours' careful selections. A few immature pairs ignored us, rapturously tilting their heads upwards in ecstatic mating displays. For me the first five minutes in an Adélie penguin rookery made the whole trip worth-while (even the seasickness!).

Not content with making sound recordings, Peter busily collected samples of vomit, droppings and urine, as well as the lichens that abounded near the rookery. Two of these proved to be previously unknown in the Antarctic.

Ted witnessed one very human drama. A parent, weary from its long trudge up from the sea, and having fed its large, fluffy and insatiable chick, evidently thought it had earned a rest. Beak pointing skyward, it went into a doze. 'Ark Ark' said its mate crossly. The tired one opened one eye and then pretended to go to sleep again. 'Ark, Ark, Ark!' It reluctantly waddled a few steps, looking reproachfully back over its shoulder, then stopped hopefully. A relentless chorus of 'Arks', however, sent it on its way, down the long slope, over the pack ice and out to sea in search of krill.

The penguins at this Sabrina Islet rookery were almost all Adélies, though we did see two chinstraps. These latter have previously been reported in small numbers at Sabrina though their usual habitat is further west and north. Adélies have the distinction of being one of the only two true Antarctic species (the other is the noble Emperor) and they breed exclusively on the continent itself and on adjacent islands. Their life history is a tribute to their toughness.

Season after season these hardy penguins return to their own bleak polar rookeries, some of which have been carbon dated as more than 2000 years old. It is October when they come back to the land, a month when the sea is still deep frozen and the little creatures, each no more than seventy-six centimetres tall, have to trudge and toboggan across as much as *a hundred kilometres* of ice. Experienced breeders return to the same nest site and construct a nest-pile of small stones (no other material is available) on the open ground. The two eggs are incubated at first by the male while the female goes off to sea to feed mainly on shrimps or krill, returning to relieve her mate two weeks later. An elaborate ceremonial display accompanies the handing over. Subsequently, during the remainder of the thirty-six-day incubation period, they take turns at departing for feeding expeditions.

Both parents feed the chicks, which, after four weeks, congregate in crèches under the watchful eyes of 'baby-sitter' adults, thus allowing both parents to seek food at once. Returning parents recognise and feed their own chicks in the group. Despite the crèche system, the hard-worked adults lose from a third to a sixth of their weight during the breeding season. The chicks we saw at Sabrina Islet were beginning to moult their baby fluff and reveal the glossy black and white coats beneath. Next month, February, they were due to go to sea.

On land adult penguins have few enemies (apart from man) but predatory skuas are always ready to steal an egg or to bowl over and kill any chick that strays from the security of the crèche. Skuas are scavengers and do not disdain a chick dead from natural causes — as we saw both at Sabrina and later at Cape Adare. The terror of the penguin at sea is the leopard seal. 'Porpoising' at high speed as they do, penguins can probably outswim their persecutors. The latter, therefore, often lie in wait off the rookeries waiting for an unwary swimmer to enter the water, when one violent shake of the seal's head is enough to break the penguin's neck and shake it right out of its skin. I once watched from *Ice Bird* a leopard seal at its grisly repast, the only virtue of which was its abruptness. To my great surprise, while the meal was still in progress, a gentoo penguin calmly swam right through the blood-stained water within a metre of the seal. No doubt this foolish one was high on the next menu.

Penguins, if they survive their difficult childhood, actually live a very long time. One young bird ringed by the British Antarctic Survey was at least fifteen years old when observations at the rookery were discontinued. New Zealand yellow-eyed penguins are known to have reached at least twenty-two years of age in their own habitat.

While the shore party was engaged with the penguins, Fritz and I embarked on an expedition of our own, leaving Lars in charge of the drifting *Solo,* which was safe in the calm water of the polynia. Our objective was the boulder slope I had spotted previously on the north side of the islet. The approach involved driving the Beaufort through fields of brash ice, which time and again collected under the boat's bottom in such quantity that the inflatable came to a halt, almost lifted out of the water on a raft of small ice. We would then have to reverse the motor or laboriously push free with the paddles. Close in, large floes were washing back and forth alarmingly in the swell, but a moment's observation showed that they were keeping their relative distance from each other, so that we could safely motor between them. The floes dampened the shore swell and, once past them, we were able to run the bow up between two boulders, jump out dry-footed, and haul the Beaufort half out of the water.

It was while I was looking for a good place to make fast the painter that I discovered I could not walk! I had no more than stepped on shore at Sturge Island so this was virtually my first landing. Now, after little more than three weeks at sea, I was so unsteady on my feet that after the first clumsy step I fell forward and crawled on my hands and knees. This humiliating performance compared ill with Fritz's agility. While I was proceeding on all fours he was scuttling up the steep slope like a mountain goat, filling his pockets with yellow, red and black volcanic rock samples and shouting all-too-apt comments about my predicament.

My balance gradually improved, though I never became fully at home on the boulders (my distance judgment was in any case impaired since a detachment of the retina, which had caused temporary blindness in one eye, a result of the traumas of the *Ice Bird* voyage). Fortunately, the extreme unsteadiness of this north Sabrina landing was never repeated.

Back in the Beaufort among the pack ice with our rock specimens, we followed the leads round to the west where we saw how a huge recent landslide had left a great scar on the north-west face of the islet. Our cameras were never fast enough to catch the penguins. When swimming at speed penguins 'porpoise' out of the water in a series of swoops (this enables them to breathe while sustaining maximum velocity when escaping or in chase). The flocks here seemed more intent on playing, slowing down to a sedate paddle, then leaping sideways out of the water onto a floe. That this was all in fun seemed to follow from their actions; after a good look round and shrugging their shoulders they would dive straight back into the water again. One that was playing this game glanced back at us while making its jump; it slipped on the edge of the floe and disappeared back into the water with a startled squawk. We were relieved to see it emerge unhurt.

Back at *Solo* it was apparent that the swell on the shingle spit was getting up. Lars, like myself, had had very little time ashore. If he were not to miss this opportunity, the sooner I ferried him in the better. The Curl Curl motor lifesavers had taught us when landing to pick the highest wave and come in on the back of it. All one needed were quick reactions, they pointed out; the boat was potentially a good deal faster than the waves. These experts are among the best surfmen in the world; their reactions are split-second and automatic. Mine are not. By a masterpiece of mistiming I managed to reach the shore in the *trough* and *in front of* the father and mother of waves. As it curled over us I realised what I had done but it was too late to save the situation. Lars made a prodigious leap ashore. The wave swamped Rubber Duck and drove her up the shingle, with me knocked flat on my face doing a rapid breaststroke in the bottom. Much chastened and very cold and wet (the sub-zero water actually seemed to burn), I scrambled out. As Dot says: 'He misjudged the waves and came in on the first of four large ones, so that he was swamped immediately and again, until he was lying awash in the bottom. Poor soul and all we could do was laugh. His language was fairly choice.'

A brisk tour of the rookery warmed me up a bit and I took half the party back to *Solo,* returning this time more circumspectly. However, when it was time for the rest of us to leave a little later, I said wisely to Lars: 'You take her. You are a better driver,' and thankfully handed over the tiller of the outboard. I was impressed to note that the Evinrude, which had sustained a good ducking, continued to function perfectly. So did the walkie-talkie once Jack had dried it out.

Back on board it was my turn to follow suit. Rather unwisely I decided to take advantage of the rare occasion of changing my clothes to have an all-over wash. Shivering, naked in the icy wind in the cockpit with a bucket of icy sea water, a flannel and a bottle of household detergent, I wished devoutly that I had remained dirty. The hot coffee and rum that Dot provided afterwards was more than welcome.

At four that afternoon, after lying-to off Sabrina Islet for six hours, we got under way again, intending to work up the west coast of Buckle Island towards Borradaile and Young Islands and attempt further landings. The configuration of the pack ice had altered radically since morning and we had to return a good way on our tracks and circle round.

'I saw a whale snorting' announced Fritz and, sure enough, a sei whale came up between two floes, blew and sounded. It was disappointing how very few whales we saw, though. The mere eleven full-sized whales that we sighted in three months were all sei and minke, small species. The once prolific southern waters had apparently been almost fished clean. The relative abundance of killer whales, eleven seen, was in striking contrast. It was not long after the sei had disappeared that three towering dorsal fins cruised past us along the lead. The killer whales passed so close that their shapes and markings could easily be distinguished under the water. They utterly ignored *Solo*.

Though the pack ice was a good deal more extensive than a week ago, morale was high and the now much-more-experienced crew were a great deal more confident that they had been when negotiating leads in close pack earlier. The barometer was high and rising. I went off watch, leaving the ship to Lars, unaware until later that a personality clash was impending. Since we are living in post 'Rum Doodle' days I will not gloss over it and, seeing that I was asleep at the time, I will quote Dot's diary.

> David went to bed, then suddenly we were surrounded by pack. Off we went in bright sunshine and quite heavy swell to find a route through. Pieter Arriens decided to be at the helm with Peter Donaldson up the ratlines. In the end P.D. couldn't stand it any longer so came down with Ted and self to have a rum. Peter Donaldson ... smoked about a year's supply of cigarettes (he doesn't usually smoke at all) all over the shortcomings of one Pieter Arriens. He really is awfully arrogant. He may be clever, etc., but he knows everything and will not be told. David and Lars both real seamen too. I'm sure he imagines he's a 1978 Magellan.

Pieter's personality constituted a real problem throughout the voyage, for he was unable to work *with* other people. During the return journey he was relieved of regular watchkeeping, which enabled him to devote himself almost exclusively to his weather observations and radio skeds — a big improvement.

On a more cheerful note, Dot went on to sum up the generally excellent mood aboard *Solo* after our two Balleny Islands landings:

> After much rum and coffee David woke up and joined us. A really super day and I wouldn't be worried if we turned for Sydney now. Ted and Peter Donaldson feel the same. We now have about 5000 feet of film shot off and some really good sequences. Jack so enjoyed his day, he does deserve it. Now we have miles of undryable clothing everywhere, socks, boots and gloves over the engine. Still in pack but David has turned us around and hopes to be heading in the right direction. Bed about 1 am again.

Well before 1 am on January 16 I was off watch and asleep again, having succeeded in reaching the shore lead east of Buckle Island. Our objective was a penguin rookery on the north-east of the island where the chart (and the penguins) suggested a landing might be possible. The same reasoning had apparently been followed by a boat party from *USS Staten Island* who had made a successful landing there in 1959 (the only one recorded on Buckle Island). Unfortunately our own hopes were dashed by surf breaking on the foot of the steep scree and snow slope that led to the rookery. There was nothing for us here, for the present at least so, after some photography, course was laid towards Borradaile and Young Islands, which were clearly visible to the northward.

The weather being unusually clear, an intent scrutiny was made of the northern part of Buckle Island in the hope of spotting signs of volcanic activity. But although, at one time or another, the whole summit snowfield was visible, never a wisp of smoke did we see.

The further we probed the leads towards the northern islands, the less hopeful the prospect of reaching them appeared. Time and again promising waterways progressively narrowed until there was barely room to turn *Solo* even by reversing the engine. The direct route towards Borradaile became completely blocked when the island was no more than a tantalising ten miles off. The only chance was to try a wide circle round to the east. Meanwhile, we were motoring through a fairyland of beauty. The ice floes glistened in the sunshine, the water between them appearing coal black in contrast. Three minke whales swam past us up the lead, blowing unconcernedly. Adélie penguins dozing erect on the floes, watched *Solo's* approach with alarm and promptly slid forward onto their tummies and tobogganed away to plop into the water on the opposite side of the floe. The sky, clear of cloud for once, was not blue but shimmering white with ice blink. It was a good time to wake the film team.

Peter Donaldson went sleepily to the rail. He had just been awakened, never an easy task, for he would invariably answer the call lucidly and then quietly go to sleep again. This time the mischievous Lars who was at the helm, seeing that Peter was only half awake, quietly turned the wheel, bringing *Solo* round 180° until the light wind whose direction Peter had automatically noted was now blowing in his face. As Lars had anticipated, the sleepy Peter had not noticed the change and the result was a very satisfactory (to Lars) blown-back spray.

Three hours were spent in filming, both Ted and Pieter Arriens being landed on ice floes at different times. After leaving Ted marooned it was some way before I could find space to turn *Solo*. It was a shock to see how tiny and lonely his figure had become, seeming no larger than a penguin, in that vast field of ice. How *he* must have felt to see the yacht steaming away into the distance I can well imagine. Dot commented:

> Ted got onto a large floe and filmed *Solo* from there. He looked just like an Emperor penguin with his orange boots and hat, with TV camera out front. We had to motor quite a distance before going back to pick him up. In the meantime P.A. also got off to do some photography and decided he needed to relieve himself. Little does he know that he was also put on film by Jack.

The possibilities of filming having been exhausted for the moment, we resumed our attempts to get nearer the islands. But lead after lead petered out, so that by 3 pm we had to admit defeat. From aloft, the sea to the north was seen to be completely sheathed in ice. This was unnavigable 8/8 pack.

There was no way through. Water sky showed to the east and there was a suggestion of a swell coming in from that direction. I decided temporarily to abandon Borradaile and Young. We would get clear of the pack by motoring to the east and, at the first sizeable iceberg we came across, undertake a detailed study of the water temperature and salinity in its vicinity. After this had been done, the ice conditions round the northern Ballenys could be re-assessed.

Apart from Captain Freeman's historic landing on Borradaile, a party from the *Wyatt Earp*, of which Phil Law, doyen of Australian Antarctic explorers, was a member, landed there by whaleboat, not without difficulty, in 1948. As to Young Island, the one recorded landing has been by a Russian party from the *Komsomolets-23* of the *Slava* Fleet in March 1958.

'Let's put up the trysail,' Fritz suggested as we laid course towards a distant berg. This was a perfectly reasonable suggestion but, since Fritz had never volunteered any opinion about sailing before, it was met with a startled silence. At length, 'Promote him to Bosun' Lars suggested. 'No, coxswain is enough, you don't want it to go to his head' I amended.

Not before evening did we come up with a suitably large berg in open water. Peter Donaldson prepared his instruments as we approached. Colin Putt, Peter and I had all become interested in the at first sight seemingly fanciful proposals for towing Antarctic icebergs to such arid lands as northern Chile, Western Australia or even Arabia as a means of providing fresh water. Actual towing techniques are not as speculative as one would imagine since sizeable bergs are regularly towed away from offshore oil rigs in the Canadian Arctic — though these are mere pigmies compared with the Antarctic tabular bergs that are under discussion. Apart from the formidable problems of quarrying or pumping the ice/water from bergs that have been successfully brought to their destination and go aground on the Continental Shelf far out to sea in 200 metres of water, questions of the rate of break-up of icebergs by melting in warm water and by calving are still unsolved. Peter Donaldson's investigations concerned rates of melting. Some of his results will be mentioned later at the conclusion of his experiments but, in general, I will leave it to Peter himself to sum up his work and explain its significance in his Appendix.

The procedure required a good deal of patience and concentration. The instruments used were a portable salinity/temperature meter equipped with 200 metres of cable, and a rangefinder. The idea was to motor to within twenty metres of the lee side of the berg and then drift downwind, taking continuous measurements the while. Six runs were made, readings being taken at depths between five and two hundred metres. Further observations were made as *Solo* slowly circled the weather side of the berg in the confused waves reflected back from its cliff-like face. In the case of this one, iceberg number one and number two, examined next day, the sea temperature was $-1.4°C$ and no diminution of salinity was apparent. In other words, the iceberg was not melting appreciably; its gradual diminution in size in these sub-zero seas was due to wave action and to pieces calving off. It was going to be interesting, said Peter, to compare these findings with those in warmer waters.

The time was now ripe to put further plans before the crew. Our original objectives had included a visit to Cape Adare on the mainland, but after the holing of the hull on January 4 agreement had only been reached (and in some cases reluctantly) to proceed as far as the Ballenys. This had now been accomplished and a wealth of geological and biological specimens gathered, which compared very favourably indeed with the results of all previous expeditions (including the elaborate and extremely expensive 1964 and 1965 helicopter ones from *USS Glacier*). Now that morale was high might not everyone be ready to complete our full original program?

I suggested, therefore, that we should try for Cape Adare, continuing the iceberg studies at Peter's discretion on our way back north. We should abandon the ice-bound Ballenys for the present and make another attempt to reach them after visiting Cape Adare. Finally, I proposed a call at Macquarie Island in the sub-Antarctic on the final leg towards Australia.

Pieter Arriens was immediately in support. For two weeks, since a change in radio operators in Davis, we had had difficulty in obtaining the satellite ice reports Davis had been relaying from McMurdo. Two days earlier an eagerly awaited ice report had stopped short of Cape Adare. Now another came in which had clearly been intended for *Thala Dan,* not for us, because it covered an area 2000 miles to the west. We were, therefore, without up-to-date ice data. 'The report two weeks ago showed only twenty miles of fast ice or pack off the cape itself' Pieter reminded us. 'The chances are that most of it has moved out by now. I think we ought to give it a try without wasting any more time trying to get the right report.'

'I was hoping we would decide to do this — go on to Cape Adare, I mean' Dot broke in excitedly, 'but I didn't dare count on it.'

'Good plan, David' said Lars, wasting few words.

'Yes' Jack agreed, even more laconically.

'Might as well start the engine and get there as quick as possible and get it over with.' Fritz's tone was resigned. Ted said nothing, but he was obviously easier in mind since our two Ballenys landings and his own little excursion on the ice floe.

'Cape Adare then. The course will be south-east to start with until we round the permanent tongue of pack that trapped Borchgrevink for a month — the poor bloke had no satellite reports — then due south. Distance from here about 440-450 miles. Take over the helm, Jack, while I look at the chart. You have to keep that low east-going swell on the port quarter. The sun, if you see it, (I glanced at my watch) yes, it should be about two points off the port bow. The best way to steer at the moment is to line up on a berg and then on the next one to come out of the mist in the right direction.' Having issued these somewhat bizarre steering instructions, I went below to consult the chart and the *Pilot Book.* I was well content. Could that near-disaster in the pack ice have been only fifteen days before? We had indeed pulled the rabbit out of the hat since then. Our modest expedition seemed to be paying off with a vengeance — and we had not finished yet!

Apart from the low swell it was calm in the shelter of the pack. Ted Rayment remembered the kerosene oil heater that we had all forgotten, disinterred it from the lazarette, wired it into place by the radio table and lit it. At once the cabin became a cheerier place. Soon the temperature had risen to an unheard of $+5°$. That night I wrote: 'Great cause for satisfaction in the way the ship's company are maturing through experience.' I thought of Cape Adare and wondered what lay ahead.

Chapter 6

Cape Adare

The *Pilot Book* was less than encouraging. Cape Adare stands at the entrance to the Ross Sea. To the west stretches the north coast of East Antarctica — Victoria Land, Oates Land, Adélie Land, King George V Land, and the rest, one single Admiralty chart covering a distance equal to that from Mexico to Alaska (this chart is, not unnaturally, a shade short on detail). Cape Adare projects out westward at the corner where the coastline bends at a right angle to bound the Ross Sea. The Cape itself is about twenty-four miles long and behind it lies the fifteen-mile-long Robertson Bay.

'Robertson Bay' says the *Pilot*, 'should be navigated with great caution. Icebergs are often aground, streams very strong, and winds often violent. Cape Adare (Lat 71°.18′S, Long 170°.15′E) should be given a wide berth. The bay has a bad reputation, as the current brings in heavy pack with little warning; a vessel should therefore be ready to leave it at short notice.'

Although we were comfortably south of the Antarctic Circle where the sun does not set in mid-summer, the season was advancing well past December 22, the longest day in Australia, and I watched the sun rise at 2 am at 165° on January 19. Our approximately south-east course of 150° would be exactly a hand's breath or 15° to the sun's left I calculated, though, as the sun moved away westward at about 15° each hour, our course and its guiding body would steadily diverge. The day was fine, the sky a pale icy blue between patches of cloud. Dotted here and there over the ocean, the icebergs glittered in the sun like sugar icing. Three seventy-foot sei whales surfaced and blew, then sounded and were not seen again.

I wrote in my diary that night of the problems of overcrowding on *Solo* and of why the Foundation's next expedition ship must be bigger with separate cabins, both for conducting different activities and for essential privacy. Aboard *Solo* 'everything — living, eating, sleeping, storage of food and gear, scientific work, radio and the rest are virtually being done all in one room. Few things have a place for uninterrupted storage. No one (except P.A. who is self-oriented) has his own uninterrupted living space,

D.L. and J.P. least of all, being homeless and mobile, using any bunk.' The final entry at midnight struck a more optimistic note. 'Have just been discussing film with Ted. Very positive now. The big hurdle, crew morale, seems to be surmounted.'

The sun rose at 1 am on January 20, after its by-now very brief dip in the ocean, in a real Antarctic pastel-tinted sky. Pools of sea water had frozen on the side decks and icicles festooned the forward railings. Two snow petrels, generally indicators of ice or land within twenty or thirty miles, fluttered round the mast. The bad weather of the Ballenys was being left behind. This seemed a different and more friendly polar ocean.

By 6 pm *Solo* was hove-to under trysail to a screaming southerly gale that drove snow pellets before it that cut like little knives. I had twice been soaked while at the helm. At least *Solo* was riding the sea like a duck, I noted with satisfaction, as I stripped off my wet polar mitts and socks and watched, with some admiration, Dot manicuring her finger nails. How stupid I had been to generalise or feel smug about Antarctic weather!

At length the glass began to rise, the wind eased and veered to south-west, the sky began clearing and we were able to stumble forward over the snow and slush-covered decks, hoist the jib and make sail to the southward, after eighteen hours hove-to. Aided by the thrust of the motor, *Solo* ploughed her way over the enormous swells left behind by the gale through veils of mist and lightly falling snow.

There was no dawn on January 22 (but in any case the invisible sun would no longer be setting), only an opalescent haze and the deck and cockpit deep with snow. We saw several Antarctic petrels. More to the point, three snow petrels indicated that the ice lay within striking distance — presumably to the west. The southerly swell persisted, evidence of clear water in that direction, and by that swell we steered.

Eleven am and the clouds rolled away like drawn curtains. Peter Donaldson ran up the rigging and immediately pointed and cried out: 'Land!' We could see it clearly from the deck now, the peaks of Victoria Land on the Antarctic continent rising 4000 metres into the clear air full ninety miles away.

By 2 pm we were twenty-five miles nearer and the whole array of the Admiralty Range massif in Victoria Land lay spread out before us in a spectacular panorama dominated by Mount Sabine (3719 metres) in the south-east and Mount Minto (4168 metres) in the north-west, both unclimbed. The sea ahead was blue and so far clear of ice.

In an excess of good fellowship, Ted relieved Dot, who had been carrying an unfair burden of cooking, and spent an hour over the pressure cooker making a loaf of bread. It was gone in five minutes. Shoregoing equipment and stores were collected. In a feat seemingly impossible for such a big man, Pieter Arriens succeeded in wriggling past the generator and autopilot motor into the extreme stern portion of the lazarette, to retrieve Dot's and my mukluks and polar mitts from where I had thoughtlessly stowed them in Sydney. 'This really does put us in Pieter's debt' I said to Dot, and she readily agreed.

Twelve fifty pm, local midnight. Sailing through smooth water at six knots, *Solo* was coming up on the twenty-four-mile-long snow-streaked promontory of Cape Adare very fast. The midnight sun hung convincingly high above the horizon in the south. Photographs were the order of the day. It was amusing to compare our impressions of the land rising before us with those of our predecessors. Bernacchi, Borchgrevink's second-in-command, admittedly enjoying worse weather than ourselves, had been less than impressed with the coast as the *Southern Cross* closed it in 1899.

Approaching this sinister coast for the first time on such a boisterous, cold and gloomy day, our decks covered with drift snow and frozen sea water, the rigging encased in ice, the heavens as black as death, was like approaching some unknown land of punishment, and struck into our hearts a feeling preciously akin to fear . . .

These sentiments were perhaps appropriate in one who was to be a member of the first party to winter ashore on that unknown continent, but the contrast of Priestley's reaction to the same place only twelve years later is striking: 'one of the most beautiful places in the Antarctic,' he wrote. (Priestley was a member of Scott's Northern Expedition, under the leadership of Campbell, in 1911.)

I have already mentioned the two expeditions (Borchgrevink's and Scott's Northern Party under Campbell and Priestley), whose exploits make Cape Adare so historic a place. Let me touch on them a little more fully.

The story of Cape Adare begins when James Clark Ross's ships, the thirty-five metre ex-bomb boats *Erebus* and *Terror,* sailed from Hobart on November 12, 1840, bound south towards the 180th meridian, where sealing vessels had reported 'a lagoon-like expanse of open water' beyond the close pack south-east of the Ballenys. Ross's aim was to penetrate into this 'lagoon-like expanse' and find out what lay beyond. It was completely in character for Ross to listen to the despised and disreputable sealers ('a sealer, a pirate and a slaver are all the same' it was said), for he had paid equal attention to the Eskimos and whalers in the Arctic — with brilliant results. It is ironic that his successor in the Arctic, the then Governor of Tasmania, Sir John Franklin, should have paid little heed to those with local knowledge. When he subsequently took over the magnificent ships *Erebus* and *Terror* from Ross, he and they and all their companies were lost in the North-West Passage.

With incredible persistence Ross pushed his tough engineless bomb ships through the consolidated pack, despite a storm in which the ships 'rolled and groaned amid the fragments of the bergs, over which the ocean rolled its mountainous waves . . . watching with breathless anxiety the effect of each collision and the vibrations of the tottering masts . . . '. This ordeal, in which *Erebus's* rudder was split and that of *Terror* torn clean away, was described by the laconic Ross as a 'trying occasion'. The vast range of mountains that Ross named the Admiralty Range was sighted on January 11, 1841. He called the land Victoria Land and, after rounding the long dark cape that he christened Cape Adare, his ships entered the sea now named after him and penetrated south to that great ice shelf that also bears his name.

Cape Adare had been named and sighted but another fifty-four years were to pass before the Norwegian whaling captain, Kristensen, made the first landing there in 1895. Among his crew was the young Norwegian/ Australian Carsten Borchgrevink. Against all odds, Borchgrevink was back in 1899 with his own expedition in the ex-sealer *Southern Cross,* prepared to do what no man had done before — spend a winter ashore on the continent. A fifteen-foot square hut and a store room, both dovetailed after the manner of Norwegian *saeter,* were put up and anchored down with heavy ropes and wire cables. This was a necessary precaution. The winter gales drove stones the size of hens' eggs crashing against the stout timbers. Ten men huddled in that tiny shuddering edifice. Hansen, the naturalist, a man of exceptional physique and stamina, succumbed to an internal complaint, in all probability appendicitis. The cross that marks his grave stands on the summit of Cape Adare.

Cape Adare has one serious disadvantage as an exploration base. The hinterland is virtually inaccessible. It was not the first choice, therefore, for Scott's Northern Party under Campbell and Priestley in 1911. But beggars can't be choosers. Pack ice had frustrated previous attempts to land and Cape Adare was the last chance. Working waist deep in water, stores, clothing and a prefabricated hut were unloaded. Borchgrevink's hut was found to be intact, though the store room had lost its roof. The new hut was set up a few hundred metres to the west.

This was the historic spot *Solo* was approaching.

Above left • **Scott's Northern Party** *right* **Carstens Borchgrevink**

Midnight had passed. It was now January 23. A flutter of excitement was caused when Pieter Arriens spotted an Emperor penguin, the only one seen on the entire voyage. Emperors share with Adélies the distinction of being truly Antarctic but, unlike the latter, they breed on the fast ice itself, not on the land at all. The eggs are laid and the chicks reared on the Emperors' enormous vascular feet, where they are enfolded by a protective layer of skin. The little creatures need all the protection they can get for the eggs are laid in the fearful cold of the Antarctic mid-winter blizzards.

Facing page • *top Solo* **amid ice floes off Cape Adare** *bottom* **Iceberg background to ice floes**
Following pages • *top* **Crew members leave for the shore at Cape Adare** *bottom* **The landing site at Cape Adare**

Top left **Barrels still standing at Cape Adare** *top right* **Detail of Borchgrevink's hut at Cape Adare** *centre left* **Provisions from Borchgrevink's expedition remain at Cape Adare** *centre right* **What is left of Borchgrevink's boat** *bottom* **Borchgrevink's hut and unroofed storeroom, right foreground. Priestley's and Campbell's hut is in the distance**

Beyond Cape Adare was a snow saddle, behind which the land rose gradually to a gentle rounded summit. The slopes were obviously easy going.

'How about that for a good afternoon's stroll?' I suggested to Fritz, 'if you and I can get away.'

'Glad to, skipper. Only too pleased to get my feet on something solid after this rocking stuff.'

My chagrin was complete when I looked more closely at the map. Me, who really should have known the scale of this Antarctic land! The 'hill' I had proposed to stroll up in an afternoon was twenty miles from the landing place. It was as high above sea level as Mount Kosciusko, the summit of Australia!

A more serious cause for concern as we closed in was the inshore pack ice that could now be seen to form a possibly impenetrable barrier between us and the land. Some enormous icebergs came into view, several of which were clearly grounded on the 'shoals reported to extend from three to four miles westward of Cape Adare'. The prospects of a landing which, hours before, had looked so bright, were now doubtful in the extreme. It was with a heavy heart that I came off watch at 2 am and handed over to Lars.

I was all the more delighted, when awakened at 5 am, to find that Lars and Pieter between them had managed to weave their way back and forth across the mouth of Robertson Bay, sometimes down the narrowest of leads, and had now brought *Solo* inside the shoals whereon the bergs were grounded and into a polynia five cables off a rock spire in the shelter of the beetling promontory.

Ridley Beach, a triangular spit of gravel cemented by millennia-old deposits of penguin guano, and a dozen hectares in extent, could be made out from the rigging. It was the site of the old huts. But between us and the beach lay seemingly impenetrable pack, which extended as far as the eye could see. Moreover the pack was moving out towards us at around two knots. Since no open water was visible in the depths of Robertson Bay, it was clear that a current must be sweeping the ice into the bay along the southern shore, which seemed a stone's throw away in that clear atmosphere but was actually eighteen miles off. After their long circuit the floes were emerging past the northern cape where *Solo* lay so uneasily.

Looking to seaward, I saw with some misgiving how the line of grounded bergs revealed more graphically than any chart the presence of the shoals the *Pilot Book* had warned against. The risk of being trapped between the drifting pack and immovable bergs was obvious. Nevertheless, our polynia seemed more or less stationary. Although no open passage to the beach was apparent, I resolved to try for a landing in the Beaufort inflatable.

Pieter, Peter, Ted and I pushed off without any very sanguine hopes. When in doubt try for the shore lead, I thought. And sure enough, right in under the beetling cliff, where the swell boomed hollowly and the backwash sucked noisily away from the ledges, there was a meandering broken passage between the close pack and the land. Time and again brash ice rafted underneath the inflatable until she was brought to a standstill, lifted

Facing page • *top left* **Pieter Arriens' ice-melter at work**   *top right* **A chilly David Lewis takes a fast sun sight**   *centre left* **Jack Pittar dressed for the helm**   *centre right* **Fog and ice ahead of** *Solo* *bottom left* **Pieter Arriens and the Stingray** *bottom right* **Jack Pittar climbs up to the radar**

almost out of the water. We blessed the propellor guard on the Evinrude, for all that was necessary was to go into reverse and pole with the paddles to win free — until the next time. I was more than grateful too for the Beaufort's stout fabric, since a bad puncture that would set us floundering in the icy water and scrambling for the dubious refuge of the nearest floe was no cheerful prospect.

Before long the cliffs receded, to be replaced by steep snow slopes and a shoreline fronted by an impenetrable jumble of massive floes grounded on the shelving bottom. Judging by the height — a metre or more — of their flotation lines above the water, the tide was low. Further out the drifting mass of floes went spinning by. In and out along the leads we weaved and, before we knew it, we were off Ridley Beach itself, searching for an opening between the close-set grounded floes.

'There's a gap!' called Ted, who was in the bow with his movie camera. He pointed and I swung the tiller and turned down the lane he had indicated between the undercut green walls of ice. As the Beaufort surged up to the shingle we tumbled out dry shod and ran it up out of reach of the waves. To make doubly sure the painter was looped round a block of ice. A group of Adélie penguins emerging from the water (this was clearly their access road too) made grudging way for us. For Peter Donaldson and Ted this was their first landing on the Antarctic mainland.

Peter wrote:

> I was elated as I jumped from the inflatable on to an icy beach. Antarctica has fascinated me ever since reading about Scott and Amundsen as a boy and now I thought 'Bloody hell, I've finally got here'. Ted seemed quite surprised when I solemnly shook his hand. On topping a small rise, we saw an almost surrealistic sight: an enormous penguin rookery of perhaps a million Adélies and, right in the middle of this teeming life, sat our goal — three old wooden huts. Walking across the rookery towards them, most penguins ignored us. Many adults were away fishing whilst the chicks sheltered in nurseries from marauding skuas. However, to our great amusement, one adult took an instant dislike to David: perhaps it was his bright red insulated suit, but everywhere he went, it followed — snapping at a most uncomfortable height. David maintained some semblance of dignity for a while but this dissolved when the penguin's chick joined the fray for a few snaps.

This last was delightful. After intently watching its elder, the chick waddled up to me with a comical air of bravado. Having delivered its token peck against my heavily quilted thigh, it swaggered back to its parent, so obviously preening itself at its daring as to leave us helpless with laughter.

Before setting out for the huts we called up *Solo* on the walkie-talkie: '*Solo, Solo,* this is Rubber Duck calling *Solo.* Come in please, Over.' No reply. '*Solo,* this is Rubber Duck. We have landed on Ridley Beach. Are you all right? Come in please. Over.'

But there was still no answer. The transmitter, tested only half an hour before, was no longer working. (This was the only radio failure on the entire trip.) There was no way of knowing whether Lars was receiving us (he was, it turned out) but, in any case, I was anxious for the safety of the ship.

'Let us get over to the huts as fast as we can and do some double-quick time filming. Then we must be on our way back. There isn't even time to climb Cape Adare to look for Hansen's grave' I decided.

The enormous Adélie rookery was far more crowded than the one at Sabrina Islet. Overcrowded, judging by the aggressive behaviour of some of the 'nursemaids' and parents, to say nothing of the obviously undesirable sites of nests on the edges of melt pools, and the legions more that stretched as far as one could see up the steep 300-metre slopes of the cape itself. Priestley in 1911 had also noted this overcrowding. Dead chicks lay everywhere, though there was no way of telling in that below-zero climate how many years or even centuries some of them had been there. Certain it was that the ever-attendant skuas were well fed, because they showed little interest in potential strays on the fringes of the crèches.

As we neared the huts and observed that the westernmost had but two walls standing, we naturally assumed it to be the oldest.

'No, that must be Scott's', insisted Pieter. 'Look at the construction of this intact hut — tongued and grooved at the corners like a log cabin, heavy half-rounded timbers. It is typical Norwegian.' He was obviously right. The thinner boarding and more prodigal use of nails in the tumble-down hut was confirmation if any had been needed. It was with considerable respect that we looked at Borchgrevink's seventy-nine-year-old hut and store room (the latter unroofed, as it had been in Priestley's day, but otherwise unchanged) and noted the intact shutters and door, the sand and snow-blasted woodwork and the rusted supporting cables. As we fossicked around it became clear that, while iron and steel rusted in the salt sea air — nails and barrel hoops, for instance — woodwork and even the unidentifiable contents of varnished food cans were preserved intact from decay.

Peter Donaldson conjures up the scene:

As we examined the amazing row of old barrels, bottles, cases of briquettes and food tins buried in the penguin guano, the old faded photographs and verbose descriptions of the inhabitants sprang to life. Perhaps the most interesting relic was half of the boat that had been wrecked and dragged across sea ice in a desperate struggle in 1899. Everywhere penguins sheltered, in boxes and even in the toilet pit. What a place to be when the ship and the penguins have departed, when the wind starts blowing pebbles amongst the desiccated carcasses of long-dead birds. Perhaps venturing here in a small boat made us feel akin to those pioneers but the sight of the small wind-buffeted huts in that desolate place with its pervading aura of death, was startling and extremely moving.

One of the most disturbing sights for me was the extraordinary fifteen-metre-high ridge of pressure ice, floes distorted and packed one on top of the other, that reared up high above the *inner* margin of Ridley Beach. Suppose we *had* succeeded in bringing *Solo* into Robertson Bay and she had been caught in *that* — to become a compressed filling in a deadly sandwich! Suppose we had lingered too long in the Sturge Island anchorage. The same unimaginable forces that had piled up those five-metre-thick floes would have crushed Solo as flat as a tin can under a steam roller!

'Sorry, Ted. We must finish the filming now and get back to *Solo.*' The unfortunate cameraman wrote later: 'I was perspiring profusely as I literally ran around trying to cram into one hour's shooting what I had hoped to have several days to do.'

We hastened to the Beaufort and pushed off. Back in the narrow leads I was not at all cheered to see that fresh pancake ice, like one-metre-wide waterlily leaves with upturned edges, was forming between the old floes. Despite its being high summer, the sea was beginning to freeze. A cold snap here could trap us.

I was not too anxious to fail to be amused at the clumsy attempts to take-off of the giant petrels that wandered about the floes. These huge birds, larger even than the smaller albatross species, were known to the old sailors as stinking nellies. All birds of the petrel family will regurgitate their stomach contents, with considerable force and accuracy, at intruders who disturb them. Considering the size of the nelly and presumably of its stomach, and the fact that it is a scavenger, the reason for its nickname is not far to seek.

Being so heavy, the nelly needs a long take-off run. We watched them careering over the irregular surfaces of the floes, wings waving wildly, slipping and stumbling and scattering the indignant Adélies in their path and, as often as not, ending ignominiously in the sea in a cloud of spray.

It was no small relief to find *Solo* in much the same place as we had left her, though in a much shrunken polynia. There was time for the rest of the crew to go ashore, but they would have to hurry. As Dot put it in her diary: 'Pack seemed to be closing in again but on seeing Jack's face, David decided it should be our turn to go ashore. Fritz, Jack, Lars and me.' It was true, as Dot recognised, that I was very conscious of the 'rewards' (in terms of time ashore in the Antarctic) that everyone had more than earned during the weary, uncomfortable months at sea, but safety was the primary consideration. A spare walkie-talkie accompanied Rubber Duck so that the party could be recalled at will.

Just as we had, the second shore party found the impact of the enormous penguin rookery overwhelming. 'We counted forty or fifty chicks with four or five adults on guard at each nursery, of which there were hundreds, going nearly to the top of Cape Adare' Dot wrote. She noted that drifted snow, seeping in around the doors and shutters, had filled Borchgrevink's hut. She was impressed too with the splayed-out staves of the barrels, whose hoops had rusted away, and with the penguins nesting within them. Indeed, there was never a box nor a cranny innocent of its round-eyed little denizen to greet the towering intruder with a belligerent 'Ark, Ark'.

Dot found the huge ridge of pressure ice that towered over the inner side of Ridley Beach as ominous as I had and was not too surprised when I radioed that the pack was moving in rapidly. The returning party found a lot more ice on the way back to *Solo,* but on the way they made one observation which was particularly interesting. In Dot's words: 'If we followed the Adélies going to sea via the leads, the way was clear all through the bigger pieces'.

In the interim we had not been idle aboard *Solo.* As mentioned earlier, when sea water freezes to form pack ice the salt takes no part in the process and subsequently leaches out, leaving fresh 'drinkable' ice, usually by the end of the first season. This ice can be 'quarried' for drinking water but the snag is that, if left to itself in the Antarctic, it will not melt but remain on deck as useful as so many blocks of granite. Pieter Arriens had designed a most ingenious but simple device to melt the ice without using extra fuel. A copper coil had been constructed that just fitted inside a large plastic container about twice the size of a bucket. The waste engine cooling water was led into one end of the coil. After circulating through the spirals, a rubber tube carried the waste water to a cockpit drain, where it ran away into the sea. Blocks of ice were packed round the coil. If Pieter was right, the warmth of the engine-cooling water would melt the ice. Now was a good time to put the apparatus to test.

Solo's bow was nosed hard into a large floe, upon which the two Peters, armed with ice saws, axes and crowbars, landed. Soon they were cutting out great snow and ice blocks, with which they staggered back to the yacht. Before long the foredeck was piled so high that it looked like a tumble-down igloo and the melting process was commenced. It worked like a charm. The ice chunks melted with unbelievable rapidity and the melted water was poured into plastic containers. Peter's salinometer came into play.

'Almost pure' he announced, and read off the figures.

'Why, that is a good deal purer than the Adelaide water supply!' exclaimed the delighted Pieter.

But by now the pack was closing in with a vengeance and it was time to recall the second shore party if we were not to be beset. Being beset — held immovably in the pack — is one thing in clear water; I had had four peaceful days of it in *Ice Bird*. It is quite another when the pack is likely to come up against an obstruction and become compressed into the terrifying pressure ridges that can destroy the strongest ship. The grounded bergs and shoals off Cape Adare afforded an excellent setting for such a drama.

As soon as the rest of the crew were aboard, and while the Beaufort was still being manhandled onto the coach roof and the Evinrude lashed in place by the rails, *Solo* was got under way. It was 11.30 am, just under six hours since the first party had set out for the shore. The next two and a half hours were anxious ones while the yacht was manoeuvred from lead to lead, always at the direction of someone aloft. As Dot says: 'It was a long slow trip out to clear water. Ted did a great job with Lars and Pieter Arriens up the ratlines. Intense concentration all the time. Of course I was, as usual when the men were worried, in the way, so I stayed silently in the stern. Made a cuppa and lay down for a while'.

Now was the time for decision. Once *Solo* was in open water outside the pack, the dredge was lowered in an effort to obtain a bottom sample, while I retired below to mull over the charts, sailing directions and ice reports and to decide on our future plan of action. I was amused to note that the compass variation, which is 12°E in Sydney, was 100°E here off Cape Adare, which was beyond — to the south of — the South Magnetic Pole. Thus if the compass had been more sensitive and still working, its north-seeking needle would have pointed a little south of east. That would be a sight not many sailors had seen!

More to the point, although we had only been at anchor or lying-to off landing places for thirty-two hours all told, and parties had been actually on shore for a total of seventeen, all these landings had been south of the Antarctic Circle on our main objectives, and one had been the first from the sea on the almost unknown Sturge Island. The collection of oriented rock samples that Pieter had obtained, designed to throw light on Antarctica's geological history through its changing magnetism, was unique to the area, as were our bottom-dredged samples of foraminifera ooze. 'Get even one bottom sample from the vicinity of the Ballenys,' Dr Quilty had said, 'and someone can write a PhD on it'. Even allowing for exaggeration, this was an indication of the importance of the many bottom samples we had obtained. Nor was Peter Donaldson's biological collection, obtained from land and sea, to be sneezed at, though I was not to guess at the time that two of his Sabrina Islet fungi were to be new to the Antarctic.

Altogether we had done well, far better than I had expected when we left Sydney. Apart from more iceberg measurements, the bulk of what we had set out to do was done. We could now afford the luxury of doing what the crew wanted most to do for their own satisfaction. Obviously, more time on shore would be welcome.

The three possible choices were to hang about where we were in hopes that the ice would clear from Robertson Bay and give us a new chance at Cape Adare; to cruise down the coast to the vicinity of the abandoned American-New Zealand base at Cape Hallet, which the last ice reports had shown to be inaccessible behind twenty miles of fast ice; to set off homeward, making an attempt to reach the Ballenys again *en route,* doing iceberg studies and making a call at the Australian base at sub-Antarctic Macquarie Island.

I put these options to the crew. Ted, Fritz and Peter were all for an immediate return north and were not even very keen on stopping at Macquarie Island. The others, apart from Pieter Arriens who was steering, also opted for a return via Macquarie Island. 'What is the point of Cape Hallet?' asked Lars. 'Even if we can get there through the ice it has been worked out scientifically years ago. We would be hazarding the ship for nothing but the chance of a run ashore.' I myself thought a return via the Ballenys if accessible, and then via Macquarie Island, to be the most sensible course.

'Sorry' I said to Pieter in the cockpit, 'you have been over-ruled. We are heading north. The course is 360° true.'

Only later did it become clear how much Pieter had disagreed with my decision. I had gone off watch and retired to my bunk when Peter Donaldson called me. Pieter Arriens had instructed Jack Pittar, who was now steering, to reverse the course and head south. This action, without even consulting me, was unacceptable. I came on deck, spoke briefly and firmly and we resumed our proper heading. Jack and Peter Donaldson thanked me for getting them out of an embarrassing situation.

Pieter Arriens, who tends to lose his sense of proportion when his own wishes are frustrated, complained to me next day that there had not been sufficient discussion. If it had not been for the need to establish unquestionable authority after what had occurred, I would have explained my reasons, especially the scientific irrelevance of Cape Hallet (incidentally, neither Cape Hallet nor Cape Adare became ice free and accessible that summer). As it was, I had no alternative but to close the subject. To Pieter's complaint that I was being dictatorial, I replied: 'This is an expedition ship at sea, not a school discussion group. Yes, it *is* a dictatorship and I am giving the orders.'

Some such incidents are inevitable where people of strong characters are forced into the close proximity of an expedition. And our expedition was a good deal more cramped than most. But no personality clash or disagreement could mar our sense of achievement. Against considerable odds (not forgetting the damaged hull) we had achieved in five and a half weeks a large part of the maximum aims we had set ourselves. We were 2500 nautical miles from, and almost due south of, Sydney. The noon to noon runs, however, told another story and were a better indication of the ground *Solo* had actually covered in her travels in and around the ice pack and in search of landing places; they totalled 3228 miles. By reaching Cape Adare, in 71°.18′ of south latitude, *Solo* had, it seems, come closer to the South Pole than any other yacht.

Having reached the turning point, there was a temptation to forget that the voyage was only half over, that ahead lay hundreds of miles of pack ice and bergs and the whole width of the Southern Ocean. There was much useful work to be done and more than one adventure still awaited us.

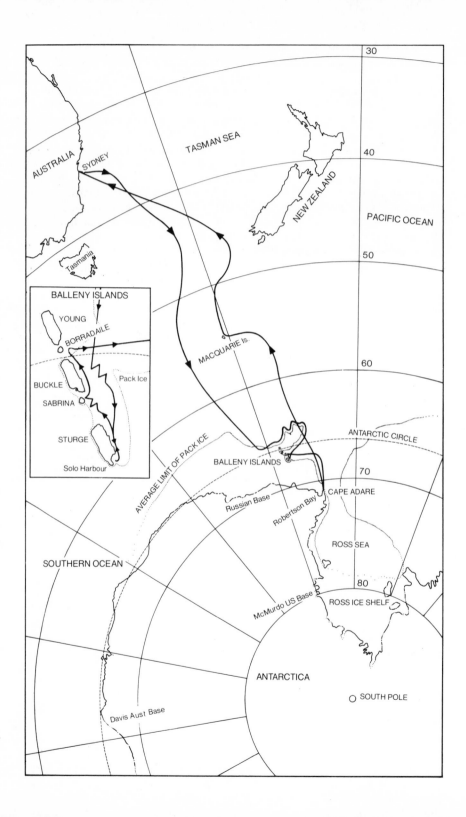

Chapter 7

Jewel of the South Pacific
Macquarie

For a day or so light winds, clear skies and good visibility were our portion, for we were still in the High Antarctic, the 'Banana Belt' of the expeditioners, where the polar easterlies often bring fair weather. These conditions were not to last. We had left Cape Adare shortly before noon on January 23. By midday on January 26, which marked the end of our sixth week out from Sydney, we were by dead reckoning, for fog shrouded the sea and sky and no sights were possible, 303 miles further north and opposite Buckle Island in the Ballenys, which I estimated to lie 100 miles to the westward. We altered course towards the islands, sailing through the debris of decayed pack and making slow progress in the teeth of the inevitable head wind.

Now that the crew were one and all tested and competent — had they not experienced a variety of conditions (most of them bad) in six weeks that many yachtsmen do not go through in a lifetime of weekends or short cruises — we went on to a three-watch system. There were two to a watch and each watch did four hours on and, unless something out of the way occurred, had a blissful eight hours off duty. Ted took on the task of organising the watches. The arrangement he ultimately came to was this: Pieter's six-hourly weather observations and the associated radio skeds just would not fit into any convenient system, besides which the met. work and the radio skeds (the latter took up a good two hours a day) were a very heavy burden on Pieter. He would therefore be relieved of regular watch keeping but would be on call if needed. The same applied to Dot. She had by now so immersed herself in the galley that it was unfair to expect her to stand regular watches as well. That left Lars and Fritz 11 to 3 (am and pm), Ted and Peter 3 to 7, and Jack and myself from 7 to 11. Since these times suited us all very well (I could take the morning sight and Lars the noon one, for instance), we did not bother to rotate our periods of duty by instituting the usual dog watches.

Altogether, as we tacked and motor-sailed towards the Ballenys, things seemed to be looking up. Lars had checked the tanks to find that more than half the fuel still remained. The position regarding drinking water was similar, thanks to everyone's restraint and Pieter's efforts with the pack ice. There was ample kerosene for cooking. The only fly in the ointment was uncertainty as to our exact position. I could do with a fix or a single position line, but the chance seemed remote, for now it was snowing heavily.

The engine was running and, taking advantage of the slightly warmed-up cooling water, I stripped off for a rare over-all wash in the unheated cabin.

'The sun' called Peter from the helm.

'Oh no!' I groaned. But there was nothing else for it. I must not miss the opportunity. Gripping the sextant that Jack thrust at me I scrambled naked into the chill cockpit. The sun's disc was dimly visible through the curtain of falling snow and, while Ted rushed unfeelingly for his camera, I took about the coldest and quickest sight on record.

'The poor skipper thinks he is looking at the equator' said Fritz, pityingly, 'but the line he can see through that thing is really the Antarctic Circle!' I was too chilled to think of a reply.

I was steering that evening over a calm mist-shrouded sea, every now and then passing through areas of brash ice and skirting streamers of larger pack. What appeared to be yet another area of brash ice came into view ahead and I throttled down to dead slow in case it should mask dangerous growlers. Not until we were right up to the little white patches did I realise that they were not ice at all but *foam*. None of us had ever seen anything of the sort before and we motored up and down taking photographs and samples. Lars entered the phenomenon in the log. 'Long lines of clusters of froth were seen. The froth clusters were about four to ten inches across, up to two inches high. Clusters were about two to eight feet apart.' The whole covered a clearly defined, elongated area of several hectares. We assumed the foam to be the product of some kind of planktonic organism but, unfortunately, at the time of writing, the scientist examining the samples has gone abroad, leaving them locked in his laboratory. We have no alternative but to wait until his return for the report.*

All through the night of January 26 and on through the twenty-seventh we pushed on westwards towards the Ballenys. The wind direction was extremely variable. Dot and Pieter took turns at the helm, the coldest and most monotonous job aboard. The watchkeepers in our new three-watch system normally did one-hour stints at the wheel – quite long enough to become thoroughly chilled – and any relief was more than welcome. Dot describes an unselfish effort.

Up at 2.30 am for watch. Not too cold, took helm from Fritz and enjoyed sailing until I did a jibe trying to avoid an iceberg, going port instead of starboard. Oh well, we got out of that with the help of a wave or two. Started engine as wind died away, only doing two knots. Came down to start off bread then took over again for a while. Lars made breakfast of sausages, egg and toast. Got the dishes done and into bed with the dough before the next watch came on.

These unassuming paragraphs of Dot's gloss over a truly heroic dedication.

'Welcome to our Antarctic playground, the new Gold Coast!' exclaimed Peter Donaldson as he emerged into fog and driving snow to take over the

---

* See Appendix I under 'Marine Samples', paragraph 3.

watch. Fog, fog and falling snow. Then of all things, rain! Still no fix. Still no soundings from the echo sounder, too deep, so no chance of resuming bottom sampling. It was now the afternoon of the twenty-seventh and we must have been very close to the Ballenys. Scattered bergs loomed up out of the mist from time to time and here and there were little clumps of ice floes. Then at 6 pm Pieter, who had been trying to get Davis on the radio for the past hour, had his patience rewarded. The long-awaited satellite ice report came through, but it brought us no comfort. The islands were sealed off behind heavy pack.

We kept on. Perhaps there was a gap not apparent on infra-red scans from so high above the earth! Before long, however, the pack began to close in around us. *Solo* had to zig-zag ever more frequently to make progress westwards along the narrowing leads. At ten o'clock that evening we were brought to a full stop by an impenetrable white line of massive jumbled floes stretching across our path.

The Ballenys were well and truly beyond our reach. This was disappointing, but how fortunate we had been to reach them early in this rather unusual season! There was nothing to be gained by waiting about.

'Macquarie Island lies north-northwest of us, but we will have to feel our way round the bulge of the polar pack' I explained. 'Let us try a north-east course to start with.'

'I will take the helm' offered Fritz cheerfully.

'We don't need a compass with Fritz around' remarked Lars. 'We only need to watch him. When we are going north he smiles, and when we are heading south he frowns.' Fritz quite properly ignored him.

It was about noon next day that we re-crossed the Antarctic Circle after three weeks. The sky cleared and I obtained the two position lines that must cross each other at a reasonable angle to provide a fix — a position. This was the first fix for five days and it confirmed that we were no more than twelve miles from where my dead reckoning had placed us. I felt proud of my navigation. But this pride was to be humbled not much later on when it came to attempting to find Macquarie Island.

The weather did not become appreciably warmer but the night of January 28 was the first occasion for over a month that gathering dusk required the compass light to be switched on. Bergs were becoming more scattered, a warning that a 'warm' water iceberg measurement was due before we passed out of the bergs' realm. A suitable subject for study came into view on the morning of twenty-ninth, a medium-sized tabular berg that Peter Donaldson prosaically christened 'iceberg number three'. (The last berg was actually seen next day in about 64°S.)

Assisted by Jack and Lars, Peter spent the next five hours making laborious and sometimes rather nerveracking runs and recording the results. The berg was in 65°.20′S, 164°.45′E and the sea surface temperature was +2.4°C, considerably warmer than during previous measurements. But the result once more was that there was no detectable diminution in salinity, no sign of melting. Wave action and the splitting off of fragments must still be the main weathering agents. The next step in iceberg studies may well be to tow a bergy bit into still warmer water and then measure its melt rate, a task well beyond *Solo,* and that must await a powerful ocean-going tug.

The observations completed, we set off towards the north once more. The bulk of the pack lay behind us and we could lay course direct towards Macquarie Island — that is, if the wind allowed us. But from now until not far south of Tasmania and New Zealand, northwesters would strongly prevail, by no means favouring our projected north-northwest course. For once the winds appeared to behave according to the *Pilot Book* predictions and we were to be plagued with strong head winds until we picked up the southerlies at the threshold of the Tasman Sea.

Not only did the head winds delay us, but the violent pitching of the yacht into the steep irregular seas was decidedly uncomfortable. Condensation inside the cabin was worse than at any other time in the voyage. Pieter Arriens took a leaf out of Dot's book and began taking his radio transmitter to bed with him, just as she was doing with the dough. One of the radio receivers joined the tape recorder, the film sound recorder and the radar in being put out of operation by damp. In a piece of gross carelessness, I managed to break no less than three mugs at one time while I was washing up.

But every day the sea provided its own diversions and compensations. Feeling very foolish, as I had every right to do, I was cheered by seeing four black and white Commerson's dolphins playing around the ship. I had only previously seen these small beautiful creatures in Magellan Strait and off Cape Horn. It was a delightful surprise to find them so far west. Overhead planed two pairs of albatross — light-mantled, sooty and black-browed, and a plump cape pigeon floated on the water. A light snow was falling. How could one be so petty as to be depressed in such a wild, lonely place?

Nevertheless, with the perils of the pack ice behind us, the paradoxical effect of relief of tension upon myself was to make me less sociable. Talking to anyone became an effort. I only wanted to retreat inside myself, preferably into a bunk with an undemanding 'rubbish book'. Thanks to Pieter and Dot, we had plenty of light reading aboard, but the stresses prior to departure had affected me similarly and I had read all Dot's books at Dangar Island before sailing. Now I was reduced to reading them again.

Warm fronts with northerly winds, falling glass and overcast skies alternated with squally cold front westerlies. Time and again we were hove-to in gales. To balance things somewhat, the compass, while showing bizarre fluctuations in deviation, was usable again. Even Fred the autopilot could be switched on when conditions were favourable. Fluctuations in wind strength necessitated repeated sail changes but, despite all our efforts, progress was slow. February 2, the end of the seventh week, saw us still 365 miles down wind of Macquarie Island, with every prospect of facing a hard struggle to get there. In this we were not disappointed, since *Solo* had to cover not 365 miles but well over 600 in the most adverse conditions to come within striking distance of the elusive island. That eighth week, it ended on February 9, should have seen us safely at anchor, but it did not. No less than sixty hours since February 1 were spent riding out gales, hove-to under the long-suffering trysail. More devastating by far, the whole latter part of the week, for sixty-five hours, we were blanketed in fog and mist. Sextant sights became more and more impossible to obtain, for to use a marine sextant, you need not only a glimpse of the sun's pale disc, but also a simultaneous view of the sea horizon, and this was what the fog denied us.

92

But the dreary week was not without incident. On February 6, a little over 200 miles south of Macquarie Island we came across our second pair of chinstrap penguins (we had seen two at Sabrina Islet), a species but rarely reported west of the Antarctic Peninsula below South America. These two birds were swimming only a very little south of the Antarctic Covergence, the junction where the cold Antarctic water, drifting northwards, sinks beneath the warmer temperate zone water mass. The convergence does not vary much, summer or winter, but it is much further north in some areas (the mid-Atlantic, for instance) than in the Pacific. The lands north of the convergence, like Macquarie, Tierra del Fuego or the Falkland Islands are green with luxuriant vegetation and ice-free, at any rate at sea level. The beech forests of Tierra del Fuego even shelter delicate little hummingbirds. South Georgia, though in the same latitude as Cape Horn and Macquarie Island, is virtually a detached portion of Antarctica. This was the boundary that we crossed around February 6. On the seventh we were thirty miles north of the latitude of Cape Horn.

The sixth of February was a landmark for another reason as well. One of Dick Smith's chartered Antarctic flights in a Qantas Boeing 747 was scheduled to fly over Cape Adare and to make radio contact with *Solo*. Thanks to Dick's generosity, Yvonne was to be one of the passengers and, if all went well, would be able to speak to us from the flight deck. No less excited than I was Ted Rayment, whose wife Anne was also to be on the flight, as was Maurice Findlay, the supplier of our radio.

As 2 pm, the scheduled time of the contact, came near we all gathered round Pieter Arriens as he tuned his Atlas Ham radio. I suspect we got in his way but he was too good-natured to complain. Right on the dot, from 1500 metres above Oates Land came the voice of Harry Hocking, Qantas' only amateur (as well as professional) operator. *Solo's* Ham call sign was VKIPA, her marine radio call sign (as mentioned earlier) was VJ6764.

'Hallo VKIPA, *Solo,* Hallo VKIPA *Solo.* This is VK2HH, Aeronautical Mobile, Come in please. Over.'

'VK2HH, Aeronautical Mobile, this is VKIPA, Mobile Marine. Receiving you strength four. Our position is 57°.15′S, 161°.30′E, in heavy fog. Where are you Harry?'

'Crossing the coast, westbound, approaching Leningradskaya. Is David Lewis available, I have someone to speak to him?' By then I was practically wedged up against the microphone.

'Hallo David. Can you hear me? We have just passed over Robertson Bay and Cape Adare. We saw the huts where you were. The mountains are unbelievable and everyone on the plane is overwhelmed by the scenery of Antarctica. Over.' Yvonne's voice was distorted almost into a squeak, but was happily recognisable. What an emotional moment it was! Yet, conscious of a 747-load of listeners on the one hand and the smaller and more intimate group close by, I could talk little but platitudes.

'How are things at home?' was all I could think to ask.

'Everyone is excited about *Solo* in Sydney', then, coming down to more important matters, 'It has been raining all the time. The kittens won't go out and they are peeing all over the place.' Did I hear someone murmur under his breath 'Just like the skipper,' or had my ears deceived me?

I said goodbye to Yvonne and passed the microphone over to Ted, so that

Anne and Yvonne ready to talk to their husbands, Ted Rayment and David Lewis (photo by Jutta Malnic)

he could talk to Anne. I was maliciously glad to see that his conversation was just as stilted as mine had been. More so; they had no kittens to talk about! Then Maurice Findlay came on the air and talked radio technicalities with Pieter, Jack and Lars. All in all, it was a memorable afternoon. We were in communication with the aircraft for more than an hour. Thinking of lights coming on and dinner being served in the great jet, we ploughed on through fog and gathering darkness under all plain sail.

Our surroundings seemed unreal — dreamlike. In a totally different way, I thought, 'dreaming' was coming to play a big part aboard *Solo*. Peter Donaldson not only retailed bizarre dreams — 'Like horror comics,' someone said — but he talked regularly in his sleep. His remarks varied from shouts of alarm, like 'All hands on deck!', to rambling scientific discourses that were much less upsetting to his colleagues. But now Fritz far surpassed Peter in a dream that was to become a classic aboard *Solo*.

A partition had been constructed down the middle of a rather cramped double bunk in the fore cabin. In actual fact the board was a little to one side, so that there was one reasonable single bunk and one extremely cramped coffin-like bunk known as 'the box'. Fritz was unwise enough to go to sleep in 'the box' and he dreamed a dream that he retailed with some bitterness.

'I dreamt I got stuck in the box and no one could get me out. Someone,' he glared at Lars, 'said "Carry him out in his box and lash him to the mizzen mast so he can steer!" You bastards tied me to the mast but my arms were too short to reach the wheel. Then Jack gave me the autopilot control so I could steer with that. Then you went below and left me to steer all the way to Australia. And', Fritz's voice rose as he remembered the final indignity, 'you didn't give me anything to eat either!'

The rest of the voyage was inevitably punctuated by cries of 'Get back in your box, Fritz!'

A rare easterly wind, as unexpected as it was welcome, sent *Solo* bowling along towards Macquarie on the evening of the seventh.

'We will be in next morning,' I predicted, with misplaced confidence. There had been one position line (not a fix) in the last few days. Lars and Peter had taken advantage of the elusive sun to duplicate my sight. I was glad, in view of what followed, that their workings agreed with mine, for the name 'navigator' was soon to be mud.

The morning of February 8 brought signs aplenty of nearby land — streamers of floating kelp, large groups of porpoising gentoo and king penguins, a profusion of seabirds that even included shore-based cormorants. But never a glimpse of looming cliff or swirling rock had emerged from the fog by the time we had run our estimated distance at 8 am, Macquarie Island must be very close indeed, but where? Was it north or south of us? We really hadn't a clue. I thought we were probably south of the island, so we headed cautiously north.

The radio brought little comfort. The Australian-hired expedition ship *Thala Dan,* which had been forced to leave Macquarie Island precipitately a few days earlier on account of a gale, reported that she was steaming through thick fog, which was reported to be blanketing a vast area of the Southern Ocean. The meteorological conditions were unusually stable and not likely to change for some days.

Pieter next contacted VJM Macquarie, who were eagerly awaiting our arrival. Had they any kind of direction finder? No. But after some discussion among themselves, Phil Pritchard, the base leader, proposed an original idea. A twenty-metre antenna would be carried up onto Wireless Hill, where a human chain would extend it and rotate it slowly to try to obtain a bearing on our position. My fancy was rather tickled by the idea of a radio experiment being conducted from this historic hill, for it was here that Douglas Mawson had built the wireless station that had first established communication with Antarctica. What I did not know was how very steep and high and windswept was Wireless Hill, up which an unselfish band of Australians were going to clamber before breakfast each morning, to tramp to and fro fruitlessly across the soggy heath in the bitter wind. For the idea did not work.

After sailing north for hours, a most dubious position line suggested that we should have been heading south. Hours later another, equally unsatisfactory, indicated the opposite. February 8 became the ninth, the end of the eighth week. Then the tenth dawned, and still no reliable clue to the precise position of the nearby land. I felt increasingly like Humphrey Jungle, the navigator and route finder on the Rum Doodle expedition. He had shown his calibre in London, where 'he had taken the wrong bus and was not quite sure of his whereabouts; but he had just caught sight of the North Star and expected to join us shortly'. On the mountain itself his longsuffering companions understandably lost faith in him '. . . since Jungle was aiming for Base Camp it was a mathematical certainty that he would never reach it'. At least I hadn't followed Jungle's example and drunk the alcohol from the compass, I comforted myself! It was small comfort. I was hardly proud to be the expedition's navigator. But what more could I do?

All this time Jack Pittar had been quietly following the troubleshooting procedures in the radar manual — which involved some work inside the scanner unit up the mizzen mast — but this was not successful. Back Jack went to the manual, alternating his attention between its bewildering diagrams and the even more impossibly complicated interior of the set itself. He had had no previous experience of radar but this did not worry him. Some time on the afternoon of the tenth, the persistent electronics expert discovered a resistor which must have overheated earlier, for it had become open-circuited through desoldering. Jack soldered the component back into position, replaced the cover and switched on the set at 10 pm without saying a word to anyone.

'The radar is working.' Jack announced quietly. 'Macquarie Island is seven miles north of us.' We had been searching fruitlessly for it for two and a half days — sixty-two hours.

Jack was, as he deserved to be, the hero of the hour. It was too late to contact the island on the radio but, in any case, a better idea was to surprise

Facing page • *top Solo* off Macquarie Island, Wireless Hill and Garden Cove in background
bottom Macquarie base from Wireless Hill

Following pages • *top left* Sooty Albatross chick, Macquarie Island   *top right* Fur seals
centre left Rockhopper penguins in creek bed at Macquarie Island   *centre right* Jack Pittar
with King penguins at Sandy Bay   *bottom left* Young elephant seal   *bottom right* Royal penguins
climb 500 feet to a rookery on Macquarie Island

top left David Lewis and *Solo* in a rough sea   *top right* David Lewis works on a chart
bottom Heavy seas

them by motoring up the coast in the dark and anchoring off the base before daylight. Nothing could have been easier now that the radar was working. At 4 am on February 11 we dropped anchor in Buckle Bay on the east side of the neck of land on which the base stands, in six fathoms, four cables offshore, in line with the leading lights.

Steep hillsides loomed dimly through the mist and darkness, but all eyes were riveted on the all-night lights blazing forth over the sleeping buildings. It was our first sight of civilisation for nearly two months.

It hardly seemed worthwhile going to bed since the base would soon be stirring. The radio operator, it turned out, was the one to spot us. He emerged from his hut yawning (as could be seen through the glasses), glanced casually round, saw *Solo,* opened his mouth in a most satisfactory yell and dashed indoors again, to re-emerge in seconds with a half-dressed wildly-waving crowd.

The first essential was to sort out a rota of anchor watches, who would take turns to remain aboard *Solo* and move her out to sea if the wind changed and exposed our anchorage. Lars and Pieter would do duty until 8 pm we agreed, after which Jack and I would take over. Pieter, who wanted to stay in some of the huts scattered the length of the twenty-mile-long island, could not be fitted into any workable scheme and was excused further watches during our stay. I forget the rest of the rota which was, in any case, overtaken by events. Suffice it to say that everyone had a satisfactory time ashore.

Full daylight revealed unexpectedly vivid green grassy slopes sweeping up through broken mist towards a plateau 400 metres above. Surf broke on the shingly beach and among the kelp-strewn rocks where great elephant seals were wallowing. A row of welcoming flags streamed out above the base's buildings. We hunted around feverishly — we had mislaid ours! No matter, a welcoming party was collecting ashore. It was time for the first party to land.

'You do the driving' I said to Lars, remembering Sabrina Islet. We roared in over the swells, crept cautiously past the twining tendrils of kelp and surged up on the shingle. Willing hands dragged the Beaufort clear of the waves and, in a moment, we were shaking hands all round and all talking at once. Ted set up his movie camera while Lars returned for a second load. Then we trooped off to the base for breakfast, passing on the way a very official looking notice.

'SCIENTIFIC RESERVE. PLEASE DO NOT FEED THE SCIENTISTS.'

Inside the wooden mess hall were Barrier Reef travel posters that did not look quite right. The palm-fringed beaches were there and the blurb, but they had been skilfully doctored to replace the resort names by 'Macquarie Island, Jewel of the South Pacific'. Meeting new people, treading a green land, these were soul-warming experiences for all of us. But perhaps the greatest luxury of all was, in Peter Donaldson's words, when 'savouring every moment, we peeled off our filthy clothes and showered for the first time in two months.'

It was Enid the cook, the only woman on the island, who now took charge of us. A schoolmistress by profession and an amateur biologist by

Facing page • Solo — aft from the mast

inclination, her warm personality made her a focus of stability among the expeditioners — a sort of elder sister, especially to the younger men.

She led us first up wireless hill and, as I puffed and blew and cursed my aching legs, I remembered the unselfish band who had toiled up here each dawn attempting to locate *Solo* with their makeshift direction finder. The rusted cables where Mawson's 1911 wireless mast had stood were a reminder of earlier endeavours. Bright green tussocks, ferns and lush Macquarie Island cabbage grew more than waist-high on the slopes of the island, but the tops were easier going, being carpeted in grass and mosses. There were no trees.

'If we climb down through that tussock grass there, and look round the corner of that big rock, you will see a sooty albatross chick on its nest' said Enid. Sure enough the chick was there, looking at us out of its big eyes, quite undismayed at the strange beings who were photographing it from so close at hand. Its mother, by contrast, was obviously alarmed and kept wheeling far out from the face of the cliff until we departed.

'Down the north end of the island we will see the fur seals, and gentoo, rock hopper and some king penguins and, of course, plenty of elephant seals in their wallows,' called the indefatigable Enid, as she plunged down through the shoulder-high grasses. The fur seals were beautiful brown creatures, sea-lions properly speaking, that were at long last recovering their numbers after their near-extermination. They were understandably nervous of us and kept well away.

The somnolent elephant seals were much less attractive, and so was I after I had fallen into one of their smelly wallows. For the rest of the way I trailed behind the party, only too conscious of my offensive odour. Then my natural clumsiness came to my aid. On the way back along the coast we had to traverse an opening ominously christened 'Catch me Cave', timing our runs between the waves that periodically surged up into it. My timing was good enough but I slipped and fell at the crucial moment so that the wave swept over me. Even then not all traces of the elephant seals' wallow were removed, for when I stripped for a shower, my jeans stood up by themselves in a corner! After a wonderful dinner, Jack and I motored out to *Solo* to change places with Lars and Pieter. What a memorable day it had been!

I awoke at 5.30 am to find that the wind had swung round to east of north and was sending great rollers sweeping into our bay and bursting in thunderous spray on the rocks fringing the shore. As we clawed off, barely making progress under trysail and motor, I thought of the innumerable sealing vessels whose wrecks littered these coasts. They had been caught in exactly similar circumstances — but they had no engines. I could not help envying the gentoo penguins who were porpoising into the huge billows, literally in their element.

The seas exploding on the outlying reefs off North Head were more than impressive and Jack and I were glad to heave-to well clear of the land. We did not get back to our anchorage until four next morning, February 13.

During the supply ship *Thala Dan's* recent visit the weather had been too bad to allow her helicopters to stock the field huts down the length of the island, and the base personnel were left with the unenviable task of back-packing over a tonne — 1130 kg — of stores 400 metres up onto the plateau and up to twenty miles along it. Having had previous experience of the hospitality of Antarctic bases, I had been concerned lest *Solo's* company should be pressed into accepting too many 'goodies'. In fact, I had spoken to Phil Pritchard, the base leader, and we had agreed that any trading should only be done through us (a pious hope). Here was a golden opportunity to repay Macquarie's kindness. 'Why don't we ferry the stores along the coast in *Solo* and put them ashore in Rubber Duck?' I suggested. Phil eagerly accepted the offer.

It turned out that nearly everyone at the base wanted to go along so, while Jack and I came ashore for the inevitable showers and the most magnificent of breakfasts served up by Enid (bacon, egg, steak and toast), the Macquarie expeditioners took over *Solo*. The sledge-kyak and Fritz's Avon inflatable were pressed into service alongside the Beaufort and crates of all shapes and sizes were loaded into the inflatables in a sheltered bay called Garden Cove under the indifferent stares of the elephant seals. The boats were paddled out past the kelp, lest it entangle their propellors and, choosing lulls between breakers, they were driven speedily out to the yacht. Ultimately every square inch of *Solo's* deck was piled high with cases.

Meanwhile Dot and I were making the aquaintance of the rockhopper penguins that inhabited a headland near the base. These sturdy little creatures with their yellow plumed heads did indeed hop among the rocks like miniature kangaroos. Dot picked up and cradled a chick. 'Dear little thing!' she exclaimed. Then the inevitable happened. 'Ugh!' She put it down hastily and wiped her hand.

As New Zealanders, we were intrigued with the flightless wekas that sidled into the buildings and made off with spoons or anything else bright they could find. They are not native to the island but, in common with cats and rabbits, were introduced by sealers in the 1890s.

The island was, in fact, discovered by a sealer, Frederick Hasselborough, in the brig *Perseverance* as early as 1810. Ten years later the fur seals had been wiped out. By 1834 the elephant seals, hunted for their blubber, had been greatly reduced in number, though a desultory blubber-oil trade was carried on until well into the present century. Macquarie is now a dependency of Tasmania, though it was formerly considered to lie in New Zealand's sphere.

Solo was loaded soon after midday and we set off, sailing fast through the smooth water in lee of the steep green hills. I was a passenger and enjoyed the role of tourist immensely. Some miles down the coast we dropped anchor off the hut at Sandy Bay, where the old sealers had been wont to take on ballast. While the heavy work was in progress Enid took Jack, Peter and me on a conducted tour of a Royal penguin rookery. These oddly named tubby creatures altogether lacking in royal dignity, nest well up the hillsides. They had worn quite respectable roads through the fern and tussock, along which they solemnly paraded in endless columns.

The foreshore itself was alive with graceful King penguins, some of whom were standing, head in air, uttering their remarkably melodious ecstatic cries. Second in size only to Emperors, King penguins resemble their larger relatives in not building nests, the eggs being laid and the young reared on their large, fleshy, insulated and blood-warmed feet, over which is draped a 'feather blanket' fold of skin.

Macquarie Island was the site of the best known of all the penguin-oil factories, and Kings were the first victims. But it was found to be difficult to extract their oil without getting it contaminated with blood, so the smaller but more plentiful Royals came to be preferred. The trade began in 1891 when Joseph Hatch was granted a lease by the New Zealand government to collect penguin oil on Macquarie. The season opened in February, when the year-old juveniles, or 'fats', came ashore to moult. Later, in March, the adult birds were taken, the season lasting six weeks, in which time some 150 000 were killed.

The birds were herded into pens, killed and placed in the 'digesters', 900 to a 'charge'. The dead birds were carried to the digester along a railed plank. There is no truth in the commonly believed story that the birds were driven alive up the ramp until they fell into the boiling vat. Each penguin yielded one pint of oil and it fetched £18 a ton.

Sparks and Soper in their wonderful book, *Penguins,* point out that, probably by accident, the taking of the birds before the breeding season began did little to diminish the total population. In fact, the industry continued for a quarter of a century without depleting the penguins until public outcry forced the government to terminate the lease − a notable victory after a well-organised campaign by an early conservation lobby. Today, while Macquarie Island is a wildlife sanctuary, there are no regulations protecting penguins on the offshore pack ice and voices are being raised at international conferences advocating the resumption of the penguin-oil trade. One hopes that this time it will not take twenty-five years to stop it.

From Sandy Bay we pushed on to Lusitania Bay, where the surf was found to be too high for a landing, so we turned back northward and put ashore the rest of the cases at the spectacular Green Gorge as dusk was falling. Up the coast one lonely light glimmered on the dark shoreline, marking the hut where Pieter Arriens was staying the night on his walk round the island. He found 'the astonishing range and abundance of wildlife to be a constant delight. I went for a walk' he wrote, 'spending two nights away in field huts, and enjoyed fine opportunities for photography. The splendour of hundreds of King penguins (with bright orange markings) parading on vividly green grass must rank as one of nature's wonders.'

That night Lars took the anchor watch and I slept in a bunkhouse ashore, the only night I was away from *Solo* during the expedition. In the morning, February 14, I made the 400-metre climb to the plateau with the doctor, Des Parker, thankful that I was able to keep up with him. The rolling green heathland, dotted with lakes and conical hills, stretched away into the south beneath streaming tendrils of cloud. We returned down a ridge that skirted the ruins of some old sealers' huts. Though the wind at the station only registered twenty-five knots, it was funnelled past the ridge with such violence that Dot, down below us, was blown over and forced to crawl.

Ted, Fritz and I returned to *Solo* that afternoon as anchor watch. A certain amount of 'horse trading' had been conducted between *Solo* and the base. We had supplied goodly quantities of baked beans, muesli and sledging biscuits, and in return received paperbacks, chocolate milk and a little diesel oil; then there had been the ferrying of stores. I felt we had held our end up very nicely and had certainly not 'bludged' on the hospitable station. Dot and Enid were busy making bread for us, for we planned to leave in the morning.

Next day the wind was fair, but it howled over the narrow neck of land with such strength that sand and gravel were sent flying and great clouds of spray spun into the air when the squalls struck and went swirling past *Solo*. No small boat could be risked in such weather, so I got out the walkie-talkie and postponed our departure for a day. The party ashore was delighted. Fritz, Ted and I accepted the inevitable and spent the day reading.

The gale slackened by morning, the rest of the crew came off and I went ashore to say goodbye. The date was February 16 and our six days at Macquarie had slipped by like so many minutes. Yet we had made firm friends none of us will readily forget. 'Perhaps' wrote Peter Donaldson, 'the expeditioners felt our departure even more keenly as it would be another nine months before the next ship would visit them.'

By 9 am we were under way and the waving figures by Garden Cove were lost to view behind a headland. Half an hour later *Solo* cleared the shelter of the land and stood to windward into big seas in the teeth of a strong northwester. The last lap had begun.

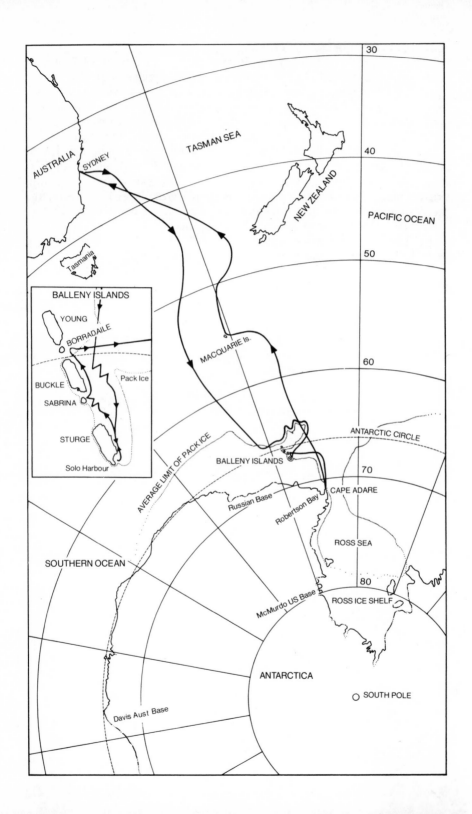

Chapter 8

Last Lap
and Next Steps

Two days from Macquarie, after treating us to one seven-hour-long strong gale, the Southern Ocean struck with full fury. The cold front storm came out of the west with little barometric warning and kept us hove-to for sixty-one hours. The wind howled down upon *Solo* at sixty knots, force 11 on the Beaufort Scale, only one point less than a hurricane. It was even stronger in the squalls under the thunderheads, when the ocean's face became white with spray. As the seas built up higher – to more than a dozen metres, perhaps sixteen – they began to tumble and break heavily and their debris of driving foam covered acres.

Through it all *Solo* rode bouyantly like a duck under her trysail, lying some 45° off the wind with helm lashed two spokes up. Only occasionally did a cross sea spin her into the wind, when the sturdy storm sail shook the yacht with its violent flogging and we had our hearts in our mouths lest it carry away. The sail itself stood firm but every one of the slides, aluminium or plastic, was torn apart and shattered.

Not only the two people on duty, but the stand-by watch as well, remained booted and oilskinned ready for any emergency. There was surprisingly little sense of motion down below, however. *Solo* would rise upwards as if in a lift then swoop sickeningly down again. Every now and then would come a roar like an approaching express train, followed by a heavy shock that sent the ship reeling, as the weight of the breaker crashed aboard. In the cabin life proceeded more or less normally. Dot made hot drinks and manicured her nails. It was only my insistence that prevented her from cooking a full meal. Lars repaired a fault in the generator and spliced a sheet that had frayed. Peter Donaldson was feeling sick again but, to his great credit, this did not prevent him from making an attempt at filming. Let him describe the incident in his own words.

Diary 18th February: Had one hell of a fright this morning – on deck filming by the mast when out of the corner of my eye I saw an enormous wave tearing down like an express train. It was obviously going to break right over us. I jumped for the underside of the ratlines and climbed as far as my safety line allowed and then hung on — I mean hung on. *Solo* went up like an elevator and the wave broke over the boat but beneath me. It was one of the biggest waves of the day. Another giant broke over us later today and wiped out some safety railings. The mizzen mast has popped its rivets and gyrates wildly ... The slides that retain the heavy storm trysail to the mast have all snapped and now the sail is only held by its three corners. If any break, it will be a desperate battle to keep the bow into the huge seas. We are sitting now listening to the banging of the seas against the hull and the screaming wind. Sure hope it just doesn't last much longer. If we have a few days of good weather and just creep into the 40s, then we are home free. But as long as we sit around down here in fearful storms and cannoning seas, anything could happen.

Peter put his finger on the worst feature of severe gales — one's helplessness in the face of such overwhelmingly powerful natural forces. They are the best breeders of humility that I know. This storm, the worst we were to encounter on *Solo,* did not leave us unscathed. Apart from the trysail tracks and perhaps the mizzen mast, it was the waves thundering aboard and sweeping across the decks, rather than the wind, that caused most harm. Three stanchions, supporting the life-rails, were torn bodily out from the deck; the metal hooks holding in place the net protecting the big number 1 jib were pulled out straight and the sail itself was washed into the sea and badly torn. Seemingly by way of recompense, the ocean left an offering in the shape of five-centimetre-long transparent miniature prawns — krill — scattered the length of the foredeck.

The seas were still wild and steep when the wind moderated sufficiently for us to get under way on the morning of February 20. Fritz looked out at the waves without much enthusiasm.

'There isn't room for the boat to squeeze between them' he remarked gloomily, than added, 'it just doesn't want to let us go!'

'It is time you got back in your box and steered, Fritz' remarked Lars, unfeelingly.

The next day it was noticeably warmer, + 10°C. For the first time in many weeks the helmsman could dispense with gloves, but the sea was still cold. It was only the following morning that all Fritz's stamina was called for. The weather jib sheet had gone overboard unnoticed during the night and was found to be fast round the propeller. Unreeving the sheet and gybing were totally ineffective; the only way was for someone to dive down two metres and free the trapped rope. Since *Solo's* propellor freewheels when she is under sail to charge the batteries, the sheet must have wound itself on pretty tightly. The sea was rough and the yacht's counter was crashing down into the water with tremendous force when she pitched. I was glad that it was not I who was to descend into that spouting maelstrom.

Fritz went over the side in his heavy wet-suit wearing an aqualung, with a safety line round his waist held by the powerful Lars. The first attempts were a failure, the yacht's descending counter crashing against Fritz's air tanks and sending him spinning far below the keel.

'That bit of string is round and round the propellor and it is all bundled up in yards of kelp' Fritz explained, after he had surfaced and spat out his mouthpiece. 'I can't get near it with these tanks. I will have to free dive.'

Divesting himself of the scuba gear and hyperventilating until his lungs were full of air, he disappeared again. It seemed as if he would never surface. Was it time to tail on to Lars's safety line? Was the diver somehow entangled? Surely he had not breath enough to stay under a moment longer! At that moment a flurry of bubbles broke surface followed closely by a Fritz who was blue in the face and gulping for air and, for once, speechless.

'All clear' he managed to gasp out. He signalled to Lars, who hoisted him, wriggling like a frog, bodily over the rail.

'The rope was four times round the propellor' Fritz explained when he had his breath back, 'and there was kelp wound round on top of that.'

'Fritz can go back in his box for the rest of the trip if he likes. He has earned it,' said Ted admiringly. Everyone echoed the sentiment.

Very thankful to Fritz, we made sail once more. Next day, February 23, saw the tenth week ended. *Solo* had fought her way out of the fifties and was some 150 miles southwest of the southernmost tip of New Zealand. Sydney was 1100 miles on and, any time now, fair southerly winds could be expected. We found the southerlies next day and the noon to noon runs mounted — 152, 113, 146 miles. Eight hundred and fifty miles for the eleventh week. All thoughts turned to home now and I began to send messages to Yvonne predicting our day of arrival.

There were few noteworthy incidents. The mainsail, repaired mainly by Fritz with Peter Donaldson's help, took the place of the trusty trysail; then the main was torn again when we gybed in a violent squall and the trysail was re-hoisted, I carelessly let go a jib halyard when we were changing headsails. It lodged up the mast and Lars, a lot more athletic than I, went aloft and retrieved it.

With the worst dangers and hardships hopefully behind us, the crew paradoxically began to show signs of irritability. 'Ted, Fritz, Pieter and Dot' were all 'picking at each other' I noted in my diary. I am sure that the relief of tension now that the voyage was nearly over was making us relax our guard. The worst incident was a temper tantrum by Pieter over having to use the radio with the engine running. I had to be very firm. This paid off and, after a day or two's brooding, Pieter got himself in hand and behaved impeccably for the rest of the trip.

Lest it should seem that I am only criticising others, I must say that my own behaviour left much to be desired. For instance, I see in my diary for February 27: 'Restless and irritable. I snapped at Peter Donaldson with no justification. I apologised'. If memory serves me aright, this incident was repeated — again through no fault of Peter's, for he is a particularly courteous and kindly man. Ludicrous in retrospect is the state of paranoia I developed at this time. Everyone seemed to be getting at me. For instance, someone appeared to be *deliberately* putting wet gloves in my sleeping bag! It required a surprisingly great effort of will to convince myself that this was utter nonsense.

Peter Donaldson has some thoughtful comments on the effect of the expedition upon our characters.

Perhaps the deepest experience an expedition of this type can provide is an insight into the nature of people and especially of oneself. A behaviourist or psychologist could have had a field day on *Solo,* although the patterns were probably predictable to an expert. It is inevitable that when eight people, initially almost strangers, are constrained to live in an area 18 by 4 metres for three months in sometimes gruelling conditions and stresses, tensions will develop. Privacy was non-existent — five berths were shared by eight of us. Perhaps any of three reactions can occur in a person: one may respond positively to dangerous situations and attempt to retain a sense of humour, or respond well but attempt to dominate others who don't. Alternatively the uninterrupted stress can play on a person's fears and make him retreat into a shell. In our worst moments we had all three types. Most fell into the first category whilst the second two traits diminished especially when we moved finally out of the pack-ice and turned for home.

I cannot better this summing up of Peter's.

Fritz, of course, was one of those who retained his sense of humour in all circumstances. He also remained firmly land-oriented. *Solo* was bowling along merrily on March 1, cumulus clouds sailing by overhead and seabirds circling. Fritz at the helm spotted a large bird that touched some chord of memory.

'There's a bloody great black crow!' he cried.

'A sheerwater' said Peter Donaldson in disgust.

Now that *Solo* had a bone in her teeth rapid progress continued. Radio messages flashed back and forth to Sydney regarding our time of arrival and, the nearer we came, the earlier became our estimates. Excitement mounted as we closed the land. But, though the yacht was rapidly nearing Australia, we were approaching the coast at an angle and it was not until 9 pm on March 3 that anything definite appeared — the loom of Sydney's lights reflected on low cloud about thirty-five miles ahead.

I went below to mark our position on the chart and then began totting up daily runs, fuel consumption to date, and the like, to be updated next day in port. The figures were revealing. Going south, our noon to noon runs added up to 3228 nautical miles, northbound to 3038, a grand total of 6266 miles, or not far short of a third of the distance round the earth at the equator. The fact that only 1593 litres of diesel fuel (out of 1824) were used in all that passage making, scouting for landings and eighteen days manoeuvring in the pack, spoke volumes for the value of sail — in terms of saving stowage space and cost. Nor did the duration of the expedition, seventy-nine days, suggest that we had loitered, despite the 243 hours that *Solo* was hove-to in gales. The longest twenty-four-hour run had been 185 miles (on December 29) and the best week (the eleventh) had clocked up 850 miles — once again, a tribute to sail.

No one could accuse the crew of having been improvident with fresh water. Making allowances for the six days at Macquarie Island when most of us were ashore, eight people had consumed 887 litres between them (out of 1456 carried aboard) in something like seventy-five days. That was an average of 1.5 litres per person per day for drinking, cooking and washing, and roughly a third of a Jack Tar's ration in Nelson's day.

Sail power — low energy technology — had been vindicated by the great distance covered for minimal expenditure of fuel and by the fact that we had been able to fit eight people and nine tonnes of stores and equipment into a hastily purchased racing yacht. That yacht, moreover, had ventured further south than any of her sisters and, in the process, had nurtured more than one ice-tempered seaman.

The cost-effectiveness of our research only became fully apparent later but, to anticipate a little, these were the main things that were accomplished.

Solo was thirty days in the vicinity of icebergs and, despite shocking conditions, Peter Donaldson and Jack Pittar systematically investigated the melt rates of three of them with an eye to the practicability of towing bergs to arid lands to provide fresh water. Peter still has an open mind on the question. The two Peters collected the first samples of bottom sediment off the Balleny Islands for marine fossil studies at Macquarie University, plus soil and geological samples from Sturge and Sabrina islands for microbiological and palaeomagnetism analyses. Sabrina Islet yielded two species of fungi hitherto unreported from anywhere in Antarctica. Marine samples were collected for the Australian Museum and mossy growths for the Natural Herbarium. The first ever seaborne landing was made on Sturge Island and an uncharted anchorage discovered.

Peter Donaldson's regular bird and whale logs possibly indicated unusual relative population densities of some birds in the area; the whale sightings were distressingly few. Pieter Arriens' six-hourly selected ship weather reports were dispatched regularly to the Meteorological Bureau in Melbourne. His system for melting pack ice into drinking water was a hundred per cent successful. The value of all our observations was considerably enhanced because they could be accurately positioned by data derived from *Snow Petrel,* the CSIRO's satellite tracking device.

In retrospect, it was easy to spot gaps in our program. Perhaps the most obvious ones were our failure to net regular krill samples and to fish consistently. An indication of our incompetence in this last respect was the shameful fact that the only fish 'caught' on the voyage was a flying fish that came aboard unaided the last night out from Sydney.

To return to the question of cost-effectiveness, what was the price of all this? The expenses of this eleven weeks and two days' volunteer expedition, supported as it was by the public and sections of industry and commerce, came to no more than $21 835. This figure breaks down as follows:

Direct expenses	$6906
Cameraman's overtime	$2930
	$9836
Four months bank loan repayments	$8666
Four months personal loans repayments	$3333
	$21 835

It might be added, on the score of cost-effectiveness, that our two full-time scientists in a party of eight was a ratio that compared very favourably indeed with that customary on Antarctic bases.

'We are coming up with the coast fast' Lars interrupted me. 'We have arranged to be met by *Cera* (carrying Yvonne and Anne), the ABC and the Customs about eight in the morning. It looks as if we will be getting there early. So what do you think we should do?'

'No point in hanging around outside Sydney Heads half the night getting seasick and maybe run down' put in Ted.

'The best thing we can do if we find we have an hour or two to spare' I decided, 'will be to spend the time at anchor off Store Beach just inside North Head. It will be sheltered there.'

And that was how it turned out. The wind held, strengthened if anything, so that *Solo* swept in past North Head in darkness and drizzle, with Fritz doing a jig on deck, at 3 am. As we glided to our temporary anchorage under the silent wooded shores, it seemed appropriate that we were to have these few hours to ourselves to make our peace with the land. Much as we were all looking forward to meeting our friends and loved ones, we needed this interlude to help us bridge the gap between our self-contained storm-tossed world and the longed-for reunions — and all the big city hassle — that awaited us.

Out at the Heads again we duly made contact with *Cera,* while the film cameras whirred from South Head and continuing showers did nothing to dampen our spirits. When we hove-to to await the Customs launch there was no power on earth that could have prevented Anne and Yvonne, laughing and crying, from swarming aboard. Then on to Sydney Cove, where the ferryboats blew their whistles and the crowd on Circular Quay waved a welcome.

Solo was home again, her Antarctic voyage successfully accomplished.

The 1977-78 Antarctic voyage was the Oceanic Research Foundation's baptism of fire. What were the next steps? *Solo* remained a week on show at Circular Quay and already we were making fresh plans. Plans for a research voyage to Torres Strait were already far advanced. It has since been accomplished under the leadership of my son, Barry, who had six years' experience as a Pacific Island trading skipper behind him as well as the single-handed voyage from Capetown to Sydney in *Ice Bird*. In charge of the scientific program was marine geologist Gabriel Sallus, veteran of the *La Balsa* raft voyages across the Pacific from South America to Australia.

But before saying more about the future, I must pay tribute to the continued dedication of *Solo's* company. With the exception of Lars, who had been offered an immediate passage to Denmark, everyone played his part at Circular Quay. This was in spite of the fact that the last thing anyone wanted just then was to sell Foundation T-shirts or remain aboard *Solo* in company with their erstwhile companions. It was fresh faces that all needed, and home comforts. Yet they stayed and helped, Pieter Arriens especially, and also Dot and Jack Pittar.

As to the way ahead, the obvious need for private expeditions such as ours is for a strengthened steel sailing vessel, a good deal more capacious than *Solo,* designed and constructed to withstand ice pressure and fitted with a powerful auxiliary engine. The Foundation's plans have advanced a long way since those March days and the interested reader can find details of our proposed research ship *Douglas Mawson* in the appendix. There is only one concept I would like to enlarge upon here — that of 'wintering-over' the ship.

Wintering involves very careful choice of the location in which the ship is to be frozen in. The bay must be shallow enough to deny access to icebergs, for instance, and the pack ice forming within the bay must not be subject to pressure — nor to departing bodily before a winter gale carrying the imprisoned ship with it! Despite these limitations as to site, the long Antarctic coastline offers a number of places, which include, in the Australian-New Zealand sectors, Wood Bay on the Ross Sea coast and certain shallow fjords near Davis in the west. The advantages of such an arrangement are obvious. The ship itself provides a fully equipped and confortable base for twelve months' research in a relatively virgin location. The cost of setting up a shore station is obviated. The summer thaw releases the vessel which sails away having caused a minimum of disturbance to the environment.

The idea is far from new. I am not speaking of the involuntary wintering of a ship beset by pack ice in the open sea. Such was the experience of De Gerlache's *Belgica* in 1897-99. She only narrowly survived, in part due to the exertions of her first mate, who was later to become the most famous Antarctic explorer of all — Raold Amundsen. In similar circumstances Nordenskjöld's *Antarctic* and Shackleton's *Endurance* were not so lucky. Both were crushed by the ice. Scott deliberately froze-in *Discovery* by the shores of Ross Island in McMurdo Sound in 1902, but the ice failed to release her and she did not break free until 1904, after a second winter. Bruce wintered *Scotia* in the South Orkneys in 1903, Charcot wintered *Français* in 1904 and *Pourquoi-pas?* in 1909, both times in adjacent bays off the Antarctic Peninsula. Ship wintering came under rather a cloud, however, when *Aurora,* purchased by Shackleton from Mawson, was swept out with the ice from her McMurdo Sound mooring by a blizzard in May 1914. The ship was severely damaged before she escaped from the ice to New Zealand.

But the practice was to be revived. The French explorer Paul-Emile Victor writes of 'a blond giant . . . the Australian John Rymill' paying a visit to the veteran Charcot. Rymill, in 1935-37, led a brilliantly successful *private* expedition in the three-masted topsail schooner *Penola* (named after his home in South Australia), which wintered among islands off the Antarctic Peninsula. I have a particular interest in this expedition and Charcot's, because I was four days beset in *Ice Bird* in Penola Strait in sight of the winter quarters of all three parties. More to the point, the *Penola* expedition was not only the last to winter in its ship, it was also the last big private expedition to Antarctica.

It is now forty-one years since *Penola* up-anchored. Since that day, rather paradoxically in view of the eclipse of commercial sail, new materials have made possible great advances in small sailing ship design and efficiency. The time is overdue for others to follow in Rymill's footsteps.

This seems to be the way ahead.

Appendix 1

Observations made during 'Solo' Expedition 1977-78

by
Dr Peter B Donaldson

Research School of Chemistry, The Australian National University Canberra, ACT

Marine Samples

Two types of jellyfish were collected close to Sturge Island. The first was gathered 10 cm below the surface in sheltered water rich in zooplankton (sea temperature $-1.6°C$), 15 m from rocks. On removal from light, this 5 cm long, compact, brown jellyfish showed rippling blue flashes of luminescence down its eight ribs.

Specimens of the other jellyfish were also collected from the surface in this area. This type had streamlined bodies resembling an inflatable boat 4-6 cm in length with two long maroon, hair-covered trailing tentacles 6-10 cm long. Their clear bodies had eight undulating maroon ribs which gave off rainbow flashes of colour by a diffraction effect.

Zooplankton samples were collected on a concentrating drag net in various localities, especially near pack ice in the vicinity of Minke whale.

An unusual sighting of froth on a dead calm sea was also collected. It seems likely that this froth is a plankton 'soup' retaining its head from a previous surface disturbance. All marine samples were preserved in 5 per cent formalin and given to the Australian Museum for identification.

Bird Log

The distribution of birds in the Southern Ocean is difficult to estimate. Current data has been mainly obtained from ship-based sightings on voyages to and from established Antarctic bases. Thus some areas of ocean have been well covered whilst other sectors have not been studied at all. As *Solo* intended to make an unusual return voyage from the vicinity of Macquarie Island to the Balleny Islands and Cape Adare, and as she is a small vessel under sail providing little refuse to attract ship-following birds, a bird log was considered to be important. This was not begun until Macquarie Island owing to the frequent coverage of this region and time spent in learning the various birds. Peter Donaldson conducted the log, assisted by Dot Smith, Pieter Arriens, David Lewis and Lars Larsen. Whenever possible, sightings were taken every two hours and the birds visible in five minutes were recorded in a number of categories, eg following *Solo* within 150 m, following *Solo* 150 m to 1 km, accompanying or not accompanying *Solo,* on ice floes, water et cetera. Details of ship's position, course and weather were also noted. Unusual species were recorded at any time. In addition, estimates of rookery sizes were attempted with details of nesting success and chick development. It is difficult at this stage to collate our results with other Southern Ocean findings owing to the many experimental variables involved. However, our sightings of Chinstrap Penguins on Sabrina Island and south of Macquarie Island support the view that this species seems to be expanding its range from the other side of Antarctica. In addition, in our region of study, Antarctic Fulmars appeared to outnumber Snow Petrels by approximately 3:1 — a result uncommon for most areas of the Antarctic. Nesting Adelie Penguins were noted on Sabrina Island, Buckle Island and Cape Adare. The chicks on the Balleny Islands were approximately three weeks less developed than those already in creches and losing down, on the further south but sunnier, Cape Adare. As is usual, we were accompanied for long periods at sea by a variety of Albatrosses (Wandering, Black Browed, Buller's, Light-mantled Sooty), Cape Pigeons, Snow Petrels, Antarctic Fulmars, Giant Petrels, Storm Petrels and Prions. Other birds, such as Mottled Petrels and Skuas were seen in the Ballenys. Only one Emperor Penguin was sighted (at least one hundred nautical miles north of Cape Adare). The bird log has been forwarded to the Antarctic Division, Melbourne, to provide raw data for comparison with later expeditions.

Soil Samples

Soil samples were collected on Sabrina Island by Peter Donaldson, assisted by Dot Smith. Samples were taken at various depths and distances downhill from the Adelie penguin rookery. The soil was stored in sterile sealed containers and has been examined by a number of scientists.

Mossy growths (the only green objects seen by *Solo's* crew south of Macquarie Island) were given to the National Herbarium, Melbourne, for identification. Dr D Horning of the Australian Museum found many small worm-like creatures called nematodes in his samples. These are receiving further study by Dr W Wouts of the Department of Scientific & Industrial Research, New Zealand.

Dr D Ellis of La Trobe University, and Elizabeth Kerry of the University of Melbourne Botany Department, have examined other soil samples. Using a scanning electron microscope, Dr Ellis has identified two thermophilous fungi. Dr Ellis states 'Thermophilous fungi have been isolated from a wide variety of habitats, usually associated with so-called "hot" environments. However, there are twelve or so species that commonly occur in soil and another twelve or so species which are less common but can be detected by persistent search. Undescribed species are frequently found. Thermophilous fungi have, to date, displayed no unusual features of geographical distribution and it would appear that they are virtually ubiquitous.

'*Aspergillus fumigatus* Fres. is a very common soil fungus, and is a respiratory pathogen of poultry; a disease known as Aspergillosus. This isolate grew well at 20°C and 50°C and sporulation also took place at those temperatures.

'*Chaetomium gracile* Udagawa — Confirmation of this identification is still awaited from the Commonwealth Mycological Institute. *Chaetomium* species have been reported from a wide variety of habitats. This isolate grew well at 50°C but only produce perithecia when grown below 35°C. No previous reports have appeared of thermophilous fungi occurring in the Antarctic.'

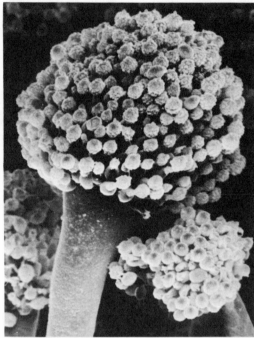

Left: Scanning Electron Micrograph of *Aspergillus fumigatus*. Magn. X 4000

Below: Scanning Electron Micrograph of ascospores of *Chaetomium gracile*. Magn. X 4000

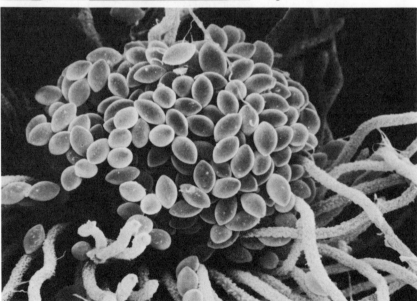

Elizabeth Kerry's report on her microbiological studies of soils from Sabrina Island is given in full below.

Microbiological Studies of Soils
from Sabrina Island, Antarctica

by
Elizabeth Kerry

Botany School
University of Melbourne

Soils were collected from the vicinity of an Adelie penguin rookery on Sabrina Island and were examined for the presence of bacteria and fungi. Samples were taken both from the surface and subsoil within the rookery and from the surface about eight metres from the edge of the rookery.

Bacteria and fungi were present in all three samples but the microbial population of the subsoil sample was much larger and richer in species than either of the surface soil samples.

Bacteria were represented by both chromogenic (bright yellow) and colourless forms; a number of different species of yeasts were also present. Fourteen species of filamentous fungi (Imperfect Fungi and Ascomycetes) were identified. One sterile and therefore unknown Basidiomycete was isolated and represents the first record of this group in Greater Antarctica. Basidiomycetes have, however, been recorded on the Antarctic Peninsula.

Three *Penicillium* species (*P. spinulosum, P. verrucosum var. cyclopium* and *P. echinulatum*) and *Botrytis cinerea* occurred in the Sabrina Island samples and are possibly the first records of these species in Antarctica.

Penicillium species dominated the fungal flora of all three soils, both in frequency of occurrence and species diversity. Other species occurring with moderate frequency were:— *Thelebolus microsporus* and *Geomyces pannorus* (both in the subsoil only) and *Cladosporium herbarum*.

The table lists the bacteria and fungi found in the three soil samples together with an estimate of their frequency.

Occurrence of bacteria and fungi in Sabrina Island soils

	Surface soil within rookery (pH 8.9)	Surface soil outside rookery (pH 8.3)	Subsoil within rookery (pH 5.3)
BACTERIA	+ +	+	+ + + +
FUNGI:			
Yeasts	+ +	o	+
Imperfect Fungi:—			
Penicillium spinulosum	+	+	+ + + +
P. verrucosum var. cyclopium	+	+	+ +
P. brevi-compactum	+ +	+ +	o
P. corylophilum	+	+ +	+
P. expansum	o	o	+ +

113

	Surface soil within rookery (pH 8.9)	Surface soil outside rookery (pH 8.3)	Subsoil within rookery (pH 5.3)
P. echinulatum	+	o	o
P. chrysogenum	o	o	+
Cladosporium herbarum	+ +	o	+ +
C. cladosporoides	o	+	+
Aureobasidium pullulans	+	+	+
Geomyces pannorus	o	o	+ +
Botrytis cinerea	+	+	o
Alternaria alternata	o	+	o
Ascomycetes			
Thelebolus microsporus	o	o	+ + +

Key:— + + + + Very common
+ + + Moderate frequency
+ + Rare
+ Very rare
o None

This study has demonstrated that the soil microflora of the Sabrina Island soils is similar to those of many other Antarctic soils. The dominance of the fungal flora by *Penicillium* species is a feature shared with other Antarctic soils as well as those in warmer environments.

Both *Thelebolus microsporus* and *Geomyces pannorus* have been recorded from soils elsewhere in Antarctica. The former is frequently associated with mammalian excreta and therefore most likely was introduced by seals. *G. pannorus* is a cold tolerant species which has been recorded for both arctic and alpine regions as well as Antarctica. It also occurs in frozen foods.

The greater concentration of micro-organisms in the subsoil compared with the surface soils, as shown by this study, has been noted for other Antarctic soils. Differences in pH (8.9 and 8.3 for surface soils compared with 5.3 for the subsoil) may account for some differences. The two surface soils were similar and penguin guano may have affected both or neither.

The microbiological data obtained from this research complement the results of a more extensive investigation which is in progress at present at the Botany School, University of Melbourne.

Appendix 1
(continued)

Whale Sightings from 'Solo'

Whale sightings are given for the *Solo* expedition from December 15, 1977 to March 4, 1978. The voyage was in an 18 metre yacht usually under sail, and included Sydney — Balleny Is., Cape Adare, Macquarie Is., Sydney. As a continuous watch was kept, it is unlikely that whale close to the vessel would not have been sighted in daylight hours. However, rough weather sightings would be unlikely (~50% of voyage). Identification was from a National Geographic chart and line charts and photographs made available by Dr Des Parker, Antarctic Division.

Whale Sightings from 'Solo'

Type	Lat. (°S)	Long. (°E)	Date	Temperature °C		Weather	Location	Behaviour
				Sea	Air			
6 Killer	57.5	158.1	30/12/77	4-5	3.6	Mod. seas, cloudy	Open sea	Near boat for 15 min.
1 Minke	64.4	164.7	5/1/78	−1.5	−0.4	Calm, overcast	Near pack	Sounded near boat and dived
2 Minke	66.1	166.3	8/1/78	−0.3	−0.7	Calm, overcast	Near pack	Moving through pack (krill collected in area)
5 Killer	66.6	164.0	16/1/78	−1.0	0.0	Light seas, fine	In pack	Passed by boat
3 Minke	66.4	164.0	16/1/78	−1.0	0.0	Light seas, fine	In pack	Diving in one spot for 10 min. (filmed and recorded)
3 Sei	66.8	173.8	19/1/78	0.3	−1.7	Mod. seas, overcast	Open sea	Basking on surface: frightened by boat and porpoised away at ~30 k, sounding and leaping (size ~50 ft.)
1 Minke	71.3	170.1	23/1/78	−1.2	−1.3	Calm, fine	Near pack	Slowly porpoising near pack
1 Minke	69.7	170.7	24/1/78	−0.4	−0.3	Calm, overcast	Open sea	Slowly porpoising across bow

Iceberg Study

We are now beginning to realise that the Earth's store of minerals, water and energy is exhaustible. Resources are not distributed evenly, so that while some areas have abundant minerals or energy they lack water. Droughts and spreading deserts are meanwhile affecting agricultural yields. Water is greatly needed throughout the Middle East, in parts of Africa, South America, Southern California and Australia.

In trying to solve these problems, many scientists, lay people and businessmen have been stimulated by the immense volume of fresh water present as ice. Less than one per cent of the world's fresh water for human use is located in rivers, lakes, marshes and underground; the remainder is frozen in icebergs, glaciers and polar icecaps. Ninety per cent of this ice is in Antarctica.

Instead of costly and energy-intensive desalination, why not tow icebergs to arid regions and pump the melted water ashore? Fanciful? Perhaps not. Between 1890 and 1900, small icebergs were towed from Chile to Peru, a distance of up to three thousand nine hundred kilometres, to supply ice before the days of refrigeration. However, the first serious scientific proposal for iceberg utilisation is much more recent. Twenty-four years ago, John Isaacs of the Scripps Institute of Oceanography, USA, studied the concept but, fearing ridicule, he did not publish; however, the editors of Time-Life decided to use it in their book *The Sea* in 1961.

Today many scientists are taking the idea very seriously indeed with an international conference meeting in 1976 in Ames, Iowa, devoted entirely to iceberg utilisation, weather modification and other applications. The major conference sponsors were Saudi Arabia and the US National Science Foundation. HRH Prince Mohammed Al Faisal, Governor of the Saline Water Corporation of Saudi Arabia, is particularly interested. Desalination currently supplies his country with almost all of its drinking water. As industrialisation of Middle Eastern countries proceeds, more water will be required. The highly polluting desalination industry is energy-intensive with escalating fuel bills approaching seventy per cent of the total costs. Nevertheless within five years Saudi Arabia plans to produce up to two million cubic metres of fresh water per day by desalination. Unless reverse osmosis desalination alleviates the situation, iceberg towing could be a viable long-term alternative.

Icebergs also have considerable potential as weather modifiers. In the Middle East an iceberg of two hundred million tonnes could cool a light breeze close to the ground on a ten-kilometre front by up to five degrees during five months. Thus substantial reductions in air-conditioning in cities are possible. In the Red Sea the coastal atmospheric humidity approaches ninety per cent in the summer: if fogs were formed from iceberg-cooling of air, then a much greater temperature drop would be likely through thermal shielding of the sun's rays.

Of the ten thousand icebergs that break off every year from Antarctic iceshelves, ten per cent would supply drinking water to an urban population of 1.7 thousand million at the rate it is consumed in London. Furthermore, this source of water could be most dependable. Antarctic icebergs, being narrow, tabular and stable, would be more suitable for towing than their irregular Arctic cousins. The projected removal of a small percentage of icebergs is considered to have little or no ecological effect in the Antarctic.

Proposals about ways of using icebergs have changed greatly. Originally an iceberg was to be found south of Chile, towed into the cold Humboldt current and floated up the coast to Chile or Peru. There it would be manoeuvred into an inlet and a fabric curtain suspended across the mouth of the cove. Pumps and pipelines would then distribute the melted water to the dry but fertile surrounding land. This simple but probably naive notion has rapidly been expanded into a global proposition. Unit costs decrease inversely with size and icebergs are no exception. Why not tow a large iceberg to other regions, say, Australia, or even across the equator to California or the Middle East?

If the scientific problems can be visualised, the engineering difficulties are frightening. Immense, fragile, shrinking masses of one hundred to one thousand million tonnes must be towed for months in rough seas across thousands of miles. But the problems have only begun: what happens when the monster finally arrives at its destination? Icebergs are usually about three hundred metres thick, so they cannot be towed close inshore. Thus they must, at least partially, be used many kilometres from land. Furthermore, the uncontaminated melt water must be delivered at a rate of at least tens of cubic metres per second and at a total cost not exceeding a few cents per cubic metre.

Before any iceberg is towed, some estimate of the rate of melting or deterioration must be known. Calculations suggest that icebergs can be towed to southern continents but insulation is necessary for longer distances. However, it is likely that these studies may not include all methods of ablation correctly.

Above-sea surface melting is probably due to solar radiation and wind-enhanced convection. Under-sea melting may occur through turbulent natural convection. This should be increased by iceberg surface discontinuities, iceberg wallowing or by release of entrapped air bubbles on melting. Calving could result from side undercutting by wave action differential melting along cracks and low density areas, stress on underwater shelves formed through layered melting or thermal stress-induced disintegration following calving in warm water.

If under-sea melting is an important ablation mechanism, then one or more of the following three effects might be detectable. (1) The lighter freshwater could rise up the sides of the iceberg with little mixing to produce a pool of less saline water. If this happens then it would be possible for meltwater to be collected in warm waters by building a shallow pen around the iceberg. (2) The lighter freshwater may entrain warmer, saltier water from the surrounding sea and thus be responsible for considerable vertical transport of deep water and nutrients. (3) Melting could occur in a stratified manner and the freshwater may then disseminate in layers. This type of melting has been detected in model studies.

Thus evidence of gross salinity variation near an iceberg would support mechanism (1), and a temperature rise would support mechanism (2). To test for these two mechanisms, salinities were measured around three icebergs in the northern Ross Sea/Southern Ocean. (Mechanism (3), suggested only recently, was not tested. The salinity changes involved would probably not be detectable with the portable salinometer used.)

All measurements were made from *Solo* using a Yellowsprings Instruments portable salinity/temperature meter (sensitivity, $S = +0.05\%$), equipped with 200 m of cable. Salinities were recorded in the open sea in the following conditions. (1) Motoring as close as safety permitted (20 m from underwater ram) on the lee side of an iceberg; as the yacht drifted slowly downwind, measurements were taken continuously. (2) Circling an iceberg (speed ~2 knots) at known distances (closest weather side measurements were at 60 m). The meter was standardised at ambient temperature before use with a standard seawater solution. Salinity data were gathered at distances of 20 m to 800 m (range finder values) and at depths of 5, 10, 25, 60, 100 and 200 m. A correction for drag on the weighted probe was not applied but depths are probably overestimated by no more than 20%.

No variation of salinity with distance from icebergs was found. A temperature inversion at a depth of 50-60 m around iceberg no. 3 was recorded but this extended for at least 2 km. Again, no salinity variation with distance was detectable along this discontinuity.

It is perhaps not surprising that there was no evidence of a salinity gradient with distance around icebergs, even in water to $+5.6°C$. It seems likely that naturally positioned icebergs are not melting rapidly or that if melting is substantial then either mixing or rapid layered spreading may occur. If only little melting is occurring this might be because of the formation of a narrow insulatory envelope of cold water. Disturbance of such an interface by iceberg towing would then increase the melting rate dramatically. Unambiguous results will probably only be achieved by using a more accurate meter very close to an iceberg (possibly a dangerous undertaking).

No salinity step structure like that observed in the Weddell Sea was observed, but a more accurate meter might detect such salinity steps in this region of ocean. However, a gross thermal inversion at 60 m was observed near iceberg 3. This thermal inversion is large for waters south of the Antarctic Convergence. Similar salinity profiles without step structure have been maintained in tanks with sloping boundaries. Rapid changes in surface sea temperature at the Antarctic Convergence were measured further north at 59°S, 163°E. The lack of a shallow warm surface layer in the regions studied may be due to consistently overcast, cold, foggy weather.

Calving is probably the most important ablation mechanism in both northern and southern waters. On *Solo's* voyage from Sydney to Cape Adare and back, 244 icebergs were logged, most of which had freshly cleaved surfaces and exhibited little rounding. However, many rounded 'bergy bits' and 'growlers' were encountered downwind from most large icebergs.

To insulate an iceberg is no small undertaking. For an average-sized, smooth, regular iceberg of dimensions fifteen hundred by five hundred by two hundred and fifty metres, the total surface is two and a half million square metres; the total volume of one hundred and eighty-seven and a half million cubic metres and the mass is approximately a hundred and fifty million tonnes. The top surface (three-quarters of a million square metres) may relatively easily be protected by insulating the perimeter and allowing the sun to melt a pool of water. Evaporation will maintain good insulation. The other sides are a completely different proposition. Nearly two million square metres of insulating material must be spread and pinned closely to the ice. It is unlikely that the cost of the material in this giant blanket will be less than one US dollar per square metre.

Proposals for attaching the insulation are varied but one idea is as follows: to protect the sides by long strips of material which could be unrolled from the top of the iceberg and pinned at depth. A huge sheet of material large enough to insulate the bottom could be folded around a drum like a venetian blind and towed to the Antarctic. There it would be sunk to clear the iceberg. After fixing one end by straps to the upper ice, tugs could tow the submerged material, allowing it to unfold. On refloating the drum, the other end could also be attached to the ice.

Tremendous problems need to be overcome before any such plan can succeed. Icebergs are not particularly regular and any gaps in the material will result in largescale melting and subsequent slabbing. Calving must somehow be contained, as the insulation would be shredded by the falling ice.

Let us assume that we have solved these problems and are ready to tow. First, we would require tugs that can deliver power approximately equal to that of the carrier USS *Enterprise*. Today's tugs are meant to operate at high speeds, so that a new design which delivers good power at 0.1 to 0.5 metres per second is needed. Bollards would then be melted into the hard snow on the iceberg top for tow lines. If the force of the tow causes plastic deformation or melting around them, a net or cradle could be assembled around the iceberg's stern. A relatively narrow iceberg would be a good towing choice. The bow and irregularities could be shaped by a hot wire as discussed later.

Overcoming rough seas, hot winds, Coriolis force (a tangential force caused by the Earth's rotation) and fickle currents, the iceberg finally arrives somewhere off Jeddah, Saudi Arabia. No cause for celebration, though, as a new job begins. As the iceberg will not pass through the shallow Bab El Mendeb Straits, it must remain out in the Aden Gulf. How then can a great chunk of ice, kilometres offshore, be converted into usable water? One plausible suggestion is to cut it into slabs with weighted heated wire. To prevent refreezing (as the interior of the iceberg will still be about $-10°C$) a sheet of plastic must follow the wire. The slices could then be towed closer inshore and melted by the sun. Another seemingly more simple suggestion involves building a narrow skirt around the iceberg. As the lighter fresh water rises up the sides on melting it would be trapped and pumped off. Model studies suggest that this is unlikely as rapid mixing or layered melting generally occurs. In addition, my attempts to detect any less saline water close to icebergs were unsuccessful, too.

The great social and economic advantages lead people to try to overcome such difficulties. A large iceberg could contain water worth a hundred million US dollars in some areas. Glaciologists have calculated that unprotected icebergs could be towed to Australia. If only fifty per cent of the water is used, the plan would still be profitable. Both South and Western Australia are in need of water. The water supply to Perth is erratic with summer usage restrictions often enforced. South Australian Murray River water is not of good quality and worsens yearly as salination through upstream leaching occurs. Calculations suggest that less energy may be expended in transporting ice to California than that required to pump the equivalent amount of water through aqueducts to Southern California. In 1977 the French consultants CICERO estimated the following costs for the towing of icebergs to the Middle East compared to the cost of desalinating sea water.

	Large berg (1 × 10⁹m³)	Medium berg (5 × 10⁸m³)	Experimental berg (1 × 10⁸m³)
Daily water production (× 10⁶m³)	2.2	1.2	0.2
Oceanic transfer costs (cents m³)			
At Aden	6	7.8	31.2
Slicing	14.2	15.4	21.5
At Jeddah	20.2	23.2	52.7
Investment required (× 10⁶ US dollars)			
Iceberg water	657.5	405.5	88.4
Desalination water	1800	1064	200

These figures indicate that, although the cost of transporting icebergs may not be great, cheap means of releasing the water are needed. Despite this, iceberg melt water should still compare favourably with desalinated water which requires immense plant and investment.

Perhaps the major companies currently interested in iceberg utilisation are *Application, Concepts & Technology Association of California* and *Iceberg Transport International* of Paris. The latter company supported by Saudi Arabia and its non-profit foundation sister, *Icebergs for the Future,* are currently planning scientific projects associated with the venture. Scientists from many countries are collaborating with them to research iceberg deterioration and movements, Southern Ocean currents and global wind patterns. These last two topics will also receive great attention during the World Weather Watch this year through the use of satellites and weather buoys. Plans are also in hand for the close study and tracking of an iceberg over a prolonged period in the Antarctic, possibly even next summer. Many other scientists in seemingly diverse agencies, such as NASA, the British Antarctic Survey, the Rand Corporation and the US Coast Guard, to name but a few, have their own plans. Australia undoubtedly has a strong vested interest in iceberg-towing proposals. Accordingly, scientists in universities in South Australia and Canberra, plus glaciologists in Melbourne, are actively collaborating with the French. Prince Mohammed Al Faisal announced in 1976 that he would co-operate with any country or group interested in the utilisation of icebergs, no matter their destination in the first instance. Australia or Chile could be the first destination for test icebergs and towing could commence within five years.

Perhaps this vast concept, which to many people is still an eccentric or absurd idea, will be a bonanza for the human race. If not, then at least much interesting and useful information about the southern seas, weather and engineering must result.

Scotch on the ten-thousand-year-old rocks could be an interesting possibility for the future!!

Appendix 2

Foraminiferida and Diatomaceae from Sediment Samples near the Balleny Islands

by
Dr Patrick G Quilty

School of Earth Sciences
Macquarie University
New South Wales

The Balleny Islands comprise a series of six islands situated north-west of Cape Adare at the entrance to McMurdo Sound, Antarctica. They form a chain, elongate in a north-northwest — south-southeast direction. Most are within the Antarctic Circle.

Little is known about the geology of the Balleny Islands and most of what is known has been summarised by Hatherton, Dawson and Kinsky (1965). To that summary may be added the reference to the volcanic rocks by Hamilton (1972) and several papers, including that by Falconer (1972) which discuss the position of the islands in the broadest geological context.

In the large area between Australia, New Zealand and the part of Antarctica between longitudes 120°E and 180°E there are two very prominent linear (but not necessarily straight) features. One is a very prominent ridge — Macquarie Ridge — which essentially forms a continuation of New Zealand to the south-west until about latitude 55°-60° when it swings east, roughly to parallel the Antarctic margin at latitude 65° when it becomes the Pacific-Antarctic Fracture Zone. Although its structure is not clearly understood, it forms the junction between the Pacific and Australian or Indian Plate.

The other linear feature is not so ridge-like but forms a series of more or less straight features in the sea floor from the Balleny Islands, trending north-northwesterly towards the west of Tasmania. It also is a line of earthquake epicentres. Because of its prominence, its linear character and its interpreted function, this is termed the Balleny Fracture Zone. The boundary between the Antarctic and Australian or Indian Plate is a spreading ridge with a roughly east-west trend. This ridge is displaced perpendicular to its main trend, very great distances by groups of closely spaced, parallel transform faults in the sea floor. Zones of closely spaced parallel faults are termed fracture zones and the Balleny Fracture Zone is one of these.

The linear disposition of the islands suggests a volcanic origin related to extrusion of lava along a transform fault. Hamilton (1972) indicated that the rocks are dominantly alkaline olivine basalt and named the Balleny

122

Volcanic Province. No detailed studies have been carried out.

Dr P Arriens was on the *Solo* expedition to the Antarctic and has collected several samples from Sturge Island, the southernmost of the Balleny Islands. Eventually these rocks will be studied in more detail.

The Oceanic Research Foundation expedition has added quite a deal to our knowledge of the Balleny Islands by bringing back several samples for specialist examination. The samples come in two types: 1) Those collected on Sturge Island, consisting of volcanic rocks. Some of these were oriented samples, which are being studied by Dr Embleton of CSIRO; 2) Four samples taken from the sea bottom around Sturge Island. All of these consist very dominantly of basaltic particles but also present are the remains of shell secreting micro-organisms, belonging to two main groups — the Foraminiferida and the Diatomaceae. These are the main topic of this appendix.

For the latter sampling, Messrs D Roots and R Russell of Macquarie University designed and built a special winch and sampling gear which could be attached to the side of *Solo* and which could take samples in water as deep as about 100 metres.

The samples collected form a valuable addition to our knowledge of the distribution of micro-organism skeletons in the sediments in this area of Antarctica.

A. Foraminiferida

Forams (as they are usually called) comprise a group of protozoans which form a skeleton either by secreting one built of calcium carbonate (usually calcite but aragonite in one small interesting group), or by binding together grains of sediment with a cement of calcite or of tectin (an organic substance). The former group is termed calcareous and the latter agglutinated.

The vast majority of forams are marine or estuarine. In the marine environment two modes of life are known. They are:

1. Benthic, when the animal lives on or in the sediment, and
2. Planktic, when the animal lives floating in the upper layers of water and dependent on currents for its distribution.

In the Balleny Island samples, benthic (both calcareous and agglutinated) and planktic forms are preserved.

The following table shows the position from which the samples were taken:

Sample	Macquarie University Catalogue Number	Depth (m)	Latitude	Longitude
1	13759	16	67°29′S	164°50′E
2	13761	20	67°29′S	164°50′E
3	13762	75	67°22′S	164°50′E
4	13760	80	67°21′S	164°50′E

Thus all samples are from some 10km east of Sturge Island.

The following table shows the main feature of the occurrence of foraminifera in the samples.

Species	Sample Number			
	4	1	2	3
BENTHIC				
Agglutinated				
?Psammatodendron sp.			X	
Bathysiphon spp.	X		X	
Tolypammina sp.			X	
Psammosphaera fusca Schulze	X		X	
Astrammina sphaerica (Heron-Allen & Earland)	X			
Reophax dentaliniformis Brady	X			
R. fusiformis (Williamson)	X		X	
Trochammina canariensis (d'Orbigny)			X	X
T. globigeriniformis (Parker & Jones)	X		X	
T. nana (Brady)	X		X	X
Miliammina oblonga Heron-Allen & Earland	X		X	
Calcareous				
Angulogerina earlandi Parr	X		X	
Virgulina davisi Chapman & Parr			X	
Rosalina bradyi (Cushman)				X
Planulina sp.				X
Valvulineria sp.			X	
Globocassidulina crassa d'Orbigny			X	X
Nonion cf. depressulum (Cushman)		X		
Pullenia quinqueloba (d'Orbigny)			X	
PLANKTIC				
Globigerina pachyderma (Ehrenberg)	X		X	X
G. quinqueloba Natland			X	
TOTAL FORAMS	72	1	304	187
NUMBER/GRAM OF SEDIMENT	7		23	8
% Agglutinated	84		20	4
% Calcareous benthic	15		77	88
% Planktic	1		3	5

Several of the forms listed are figured elsewhere. *Globocassidulina crassa* is by far the most abundant species comprising 74 and 80% of the total fauna in samples 2 and 3. The planktic percentage is low as is expected in shallow samples, but may be a little lower than expected for the deeper samples. *Globigerina pachyderma* is the only planktic form usually to be expected so far south. The presence of the other species seems anomalous.

Echols and Kennett (1973) have collated the information gleaned from hundreds of samples taken in the circum-Antarctic area, including four north-west and west of Young Island and one somewhat south of Sturge Island. Those samples usually are more than 50 per cent agglutinated but the results are not very comparable because all those samples were taken from more than 2000 m water depth. In the greater depth, the absence of calcareous forms results from dissolution of calcium carbonate below the calcite compensation depth (CCD) which is shallower in polar regions than elsewhere.

Forams are illustrated using a Scanning Electron Microscope at Macquarie University.

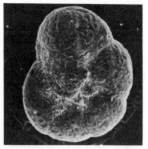

Trochammina nana (Brady) X 250

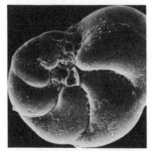

Miliammina oblonga
Heron-Allen & Earland X 250

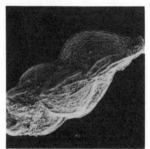

Angulogerina earlandi X 120

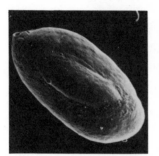

Valvulineria sp X 300

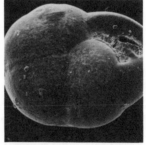

Globocassidulina crassa X 150

Pullenia quinqueloba X 230

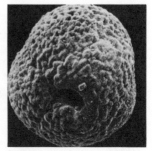

Globigerina pachyderma X 300

125

B. Diatomaceae

Diatoms are a group of small unicellular plants which secrete a beautiful skeleton of opaline silica. They are one of the most important life forms on earth as they account for 20-25 per cent of the world's total photosynthesis, the source of the oxygen we breathe.

They inhabit an extremely diverse range of aqueous habitats including the ocean, all freshwaters and such places as fountains, poorly tended backyard swimming pools and water supplies.

Because of the high nutrient content of Antarctic waters, diatoms are extremely abundant and because of the composition of the skeleton, they are important elements of sediments accumulating there.

The skeleton consists of two shells or valves, one of which is slightly larger than the other so that they fit together. The plant consists of single isolated cells or of chains of cells up to 1 cm long. Like forams, there are both benthic and planktic forms.

Mr Howard Brady of Macquarie University has had a great deal of experience with Antarctic diatoms and has identified the following forms from Sample No. 3.

Amphora sp. ($<1\%$)
Coscinodiscus lentiginosus (Janisch) Hasle ($<1\%$)
Diploneis spp. (1.5%)
Melosira sol (Ehrenberg)
Nitzschia angulata (O'Meara) Hasle (9%)
N. curta (Van Huerck) Hasle (35%)
N. cylindrus (Grunow) Hasle (20%)
N. ritscheri (Hustedt) Hasle ($<1\%$)
N. kerguelensis (O'Meara) Hasle ($<1\%$)
Navicula sp. 1 (8%)
N. (small species) (8%)
Tracyneis aspra (Ehrenberg) Cleve (4%)
Thalassiosira sp. ($<1\%$)
Eucampia balaustium Castracane ($<1\%$)

The sample studied is reckoned to be the only one suitable for diatom analysis although some diatoms also occur in other samples. Benthic forms make up about 20% of the flora, perhaps reflecting a lower incidence of pack ice conditions than in comparable depths farther south, for example Ross Island in McMurdo Sound.

Diatoms are illustrated using a high quality light microscope with oil immersion lenses and Nomarski phase interference system.

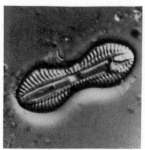

Diploneis spp 1 X 500

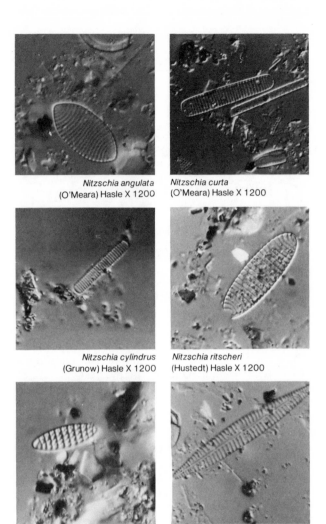

Nitzschia angulata
(O'Meara) Hasle X 1200

Nitzschia curta
(O'Meara) Hasle X 1200

Nitzschia cylindrus
(Grunow) Hasle X 1200

Nitzschia ritscheri
(Hustedt) Hasle X 1200

Nitzschia kerguelensis
(O'Meara) Hasle X 1200

Navicula spp X 1200

References

Echols, RJ and Kennett, JP, 1973. Distribution of foraminifera in the surface sediments. In Bushnell, V (Editor) Marine sediments of the Southern Oceans, American Geographical Society, Antarctic map folio series no. 17, pages 13-17.

Falconer, RKH, 1972. The Indian-Antarctic-Pacific triple junction. Earth and Planetary Science Letters, Volume 7, pages 151-158.

Hamilton, W, 1972. The Hallett Volcanic Province, Antarctica. Professional Papers of the United States Geological Survey, No. 456-C, pages C1-C61.

Hatherton, T, Dawson, EW and Kinsky, FC, 1965. Balleny Islands Reconnaissance Expedition, 1964. New Zealand Journal of Geology and Geophysics, Volume 8, pages 164-179.

Appendix 3

Magnetic Properties of Oriented Rock Samples from Sturge Island and Sabrina Island in the Balleny Group

by
Dr BJJ Embleton

CSIRO Division of Mineral Physics
New South Wales

Three oriented samples of basalt were collected by Dr PA Arriens at the brief stops during *Solo*'s passage through the Balleny Islands. I believe these to represent the first oriented rock samples from *in situ* basalt outcrop to be collected in these Islands. One sample was taken from Sturge Island and two samples from the base of the Monolith (a 100 m high spire of volcanic rock) tied to Sabrina Island by a gravel isthmus.

Cores, 25 mm diameter, were drilled out of the samples and then sliced into specimens 22 mm long. Their remanent magnetisations and susceptibilities were measured on a DIGICO Complete Results Magnetometer (Molyneux, 1971). The stability of magnetisation to alternating field (AF) and thermal treatment was tested following the methods described by Collinson *et al* (1967).

It was recognised that sample orientation with a magnetic compass is somewhat less than ideal since (a) the basalts themselves are sufficiently magnetic to possibly deflect a compass needle, and (b) the sampling localities (Sturge Island at approximately 67.5°S, 164.7°E and Sabrina Island at 66.9°S, 163.1°E) were relatively close to the south magnetic pole (at approximately 66°S, 138°E) so that the period of the compass needle was about 15 seconds. Though sun compass readings were recorded they were equivocal. However, it will be shown that the magnetic compass readings for the two samples from Sabrina Island provide consistent results.

One specimen from each sample was selected for detailed investigation of its magnetic stability in alternating fields and one specimen from each sample for detailed thermal demagnetisation tests.

Sturge Island
Field Number: S1
Macquarie University catalogue number: MU 13723

Directions of natural remanent magnetisation (NRM) were scattered and negative, ie upward pointing which is normal for a present day southern hemisphere magnetisation. Average values of direction, intensity and

128

magnetic susceptibility are listed in Table 1. Alternating magnetic field treatment isolated a harder, stable component of magnetisation which is downward pointing – see Table 2. This is a reversed direction of magnetisation and was acquired when the earth's magnetic field held reversed polarity. The superimposed (overprinted) upward pointing component was acquired after the rock was formed and is a low coercive force, soft magnetisation. Indeed, a proportion of the grains that carry the remanence are multidomain and care had to be taken during experimental work to prevent spurious magnetisations influencing the directions obtained after thermal and AF cleaning.

Sabrina Island
Field Numbers: M1, M2
Macquarie University catalogue numbers: MU 13713, MU 13714 respectively.

Average values of the natural remanent magnetisation and magnetic susceptibility are given in Table 1. The NRM directions are tightly grouped within samples, and AF cleaning produced only a minor shift in direction though clearly demonstrated that the magnetisations have normal polarity – shown in Table 2. Since only three specimens could be cut from sample MU 13714 (M2), and one specimen was used for thermal demagnetisation, the cleaned results from that specimen were combined with the AF results from two specimens to yield an average direction for the sample.

Conclusions

Average directions of magnetisation in the two samples from Sabrina Island obtained after AF and thermal cleaning are very close (Table 2), thus providing some justification for using the magnetic orientation data. Sample orientations are (a) for MU 13713 (M1); strike = 304° true north, dip = 51°SW and (b) for MU 13714 (M2); strike = 004° true north, dip = 81°W.

The mean of the three sample average directions of magnetisation (using the antiparallel direction for sample MU 13723 (S1)) is declination = 266°, inclination = $-64°$, $\alpha 95 = 18°$ and the average south virtual geomagnetic pole lies at Latitude = 41°S, Longitude = 228°E, $\alpha 95 = 25°$. Interestingly, this pole lies close to the group of poles obtained previously from studies of the Jurassic Ferrar Dolerite from Antarctica; these data are reviewed by McElhinny (1973), who gives an average Jurassic pole at 53°S, 215°E.

I should like to take this opportunity to express my gratitude to David Lewis and Pieter Arriens for kindly making these unique samples available for study.

Discussion

The Balleny Islands comprise a chain of volcanoes, mainly extinct, which trend approximately NW-SE for a distance of about 160 kilometres, and lie about 200 kilometres from the Antarctic coast. In 1839, Balleny reported volcanic activity on Buckle Island but during two subsequent expeditions in the 1930s, no sign of activity was observed. If the Ballenys form a chain analogous to the volcanic chains in the Pacific Ocean (such as the Hawaiian Islands and the Society Islands), we may expect to see a systematic variation in age with the distance along the length of the Island chain. The radiometric age of one sample from Sturge Island (the most southerly of the chain) indicates activity there at 1.91 million years. Activity on Sabrina

Island (at the southern tip of Buckle Island and the next island in the chain) is now documented at 558 000 years, and activity has actually been observed on Buckle Island. Just how Borradaile, Row and Young Islands (moving progressively northwards) fit this pattern of igneous activity will remain unresolved until estimates of their ages are available. On a simple model of oceanic crust in uniform relative motion over a volcanic source, the ages may be expected to young northwards.

The results from the magnetic work are also puzzling in the light of the youthfulness of the Islands. It is premature to speculate on these results since the present collection is relatively small. However, the polarities of magnetisation do conform with the known polarity history of the geomagnetic field for the Tertiary Period and the polarities measured are approximately antiparallel. However, why there should be a large angular divergence of the directions from the present best fitting dipole field direction, also remains unresolved.

References

Collinson, DW, Creer, KM and Runcorn, SK, 1967. Methods in Palaeomagnetism. Elsevier, Amsterdam, 609 p.

Fisher, RA, 1953. Dispersion on a sphere. Proc. Roy. Soc. London, *217A*, 295-305.

McElhinny, MW, 1973. Palaeomagnetism and Plate Tectonics. Cambridge University Press, 358 p.

Molyneux, L, 1971. A complete results magnetometer for measuring the remanent magnetisation of rocks. Geophys. J. Roy. Astr. Soc., *24*, 429-433.

TABLE 1

Properties of Natural Remanent Magnetisation of Samples from Sturge Island (S) and the Monolith at Sabrina Island (M) in the Balleny Group

Sample	N	K	Dec	Inc	α95	Int ± SD	EMU Vol. Susc ± SD
MU 13713 (M1)	9	1502	262°	−63°	1.3°	7477 ± 326	3473 ± 295
MU 13714 (M2)	3	7775	265°	−54°	1.3°	7312 ± 391	3012 ± 49
MU 13723 (S1)	17	9.6	134°	−66°	12.1°	902 ± 203	4120 ± 177

Notes to Table 1

N = number of specimens cut from each sample

K = a precision parameter describing the amount of scatter in the directions of magnetisation, defined by Fisher (1953)

Dec = declination, measured east positive

Inc = inclination, negative is upward pointing and positive is downward pointing

α95 = half angle of the cone of confidence calculated at the 95% probability level (Fisher, 1953)

Int ± SD = average intensity of magnetisation in units of gauss (mAm^{-1}SI) ± standard deviation

Susc ± SD = average magnetic susceptibility ± standard deviation

TABLE 2

Summary of Directional Changes during Partial Demagnetisation of Samples from Sturge Island (S) and Sabrina Island (M)

Sample	Treatment	N	K	Dec	Inc	α95
MU 13713 (M1)	NRM	3	864	259°	−63°	4.1°
	10mT AF	3	977	266°	−57°	3.9°
	20mT AF	3	934	262°	−57°	4.0°
MU 13714 (M2)	NRM	3	7775	265°	−54°	1.3°
	10mT AF and 200°C	3	602	267°	−58°	5.0°
	20mT AF and 300°C	3	1081	267°	−57°	3.7°
MU 13723 (S1)	NRM	3	5	148°	−67°	61.0°
	15mT AF	3	456	103°	+77°	5.7°
	20mT AF	3	873	092°	+77°	4.1°

Notes to Table 2

N   = number of specimens

K   = precision parameter (see notes to Table 1)

Dec   = declination

Inc   = inclination

α95   = half angle of the cone of confidence at the 95% probability level

Appendix 4

The Electrical Side of Solo

by
Jack Pittar

Vic Meyers was an innovative man, and the boat's electrical features reflected this. Much of the equipment, however, needed attention.

Due to the overcrowding and storage of equipment in the cabin (above and below the floorboards) an enormous effort to carry out even simple tasks was required. Heavy clothing, movement of the boat, a busy schedule of watches, cooking, and radio reports all forced maintenance to be kept to the essential. It should have all been prepared before we left, but the time just wasn't there. Ninety per cent of any voyage is in the preparation.

The easiest way to discuss the equipment is piece by piece:

Bilge Light
As the water level in the bilge rises, air trapped in a pipe leading into the bilge increases in pressure. On the top end of this pipe is an air-pressure switch normally used in automatic washing machines. At a certain pressure (or water level) this switch turns on a large red light in the cabin to give a clear and early warning of the rising water.

All the batteries and most of our supplies were kept below the floorboards. It is all too easy to forget the occasional test-pump, and it was impossible to just look into the bilge occasionally. After the ice-damage to the hull, water ingress would not have been detected by either of these means. Without the simple bilge light many of our stores would have been ruined.

Sailing Generator
A most interesting device. While under sail a lever is pulled to disengage the motor and to connect the propellor, via the prop shaft, to an automotive generator through a gearing up system. At four knots the generator starts charging the domestic batteries. At six knots a healthy seven amps pours into the 24 volt domestic system. The motor was not needed between Sydney and the ice for charging.

Domestic Electrical System
There were two massive 180 Ampere hour 12 volt batteries wired in series that could be charged from the sailing generator, or an auxiliary generator

on the main motor, or from a petrol generator under the cockpit.

The sheet winches were electric without a manual option. We knew a manual backup was essential, but there wasn't time to prepare it. Internal lighting consisted of flourescent lights which proved only semi-reliable and hard to get parts for. Radar, echo sounder, radio batteries, navigation lights, and the self steering system were all powered from this domestic battery system.

Starting System

This comprised the normal diesel's generator charging only the separate starter batteries. There was no provision for manual starting.

Radio System

We chose a 100 watt PEP single sideband Stingray radio, but when it came down to it, we just couldn't afford it. Mr Findlay of Findlay Electronics Ltd then kindly offered us the loan of two sets.

With only two weeks left until the date of departure all the crystals had to be rushed from Singapore (Australian producers had trouble supplying), installed in the radios, and the radios tested for temperature, humidity and stability. The radios were installed in *Solo* two days before departure. Because two Radphone frequencies had been added, some modifications to the aerials became necessary. Mr Findlay was busy until 6am the morning of departure. The PMG people examined Lars Larsen, Pieter Arriens and myself for licences on the quay-side that morning.

The frequencies we used were suitable for the new Coastal Radio Network. These were 2mHz AM emergency channel, 4 and 6mHz calling and duplex frequencies, and 13mHz duplex Radphone. Some other crystals had been installed for communication with the Antarctic stations. A 20-metre aerial which ran between the masts and down to the cabin was used for the emergency channel, and a 4-metre aerial from the cabin up to the mizzen mast was used for the remaining frequencies. Marine Stingray radios came with a separate automatic tuning unit which proved to be a godsend. It automatically connected to the appropriate aerial and no aerial tuning by the operator was required. Since Radio Melbourne and Radio Sydney were just having the new frequencies installed we sometimes communicated by talking to one on one frequency, and receiving from the other on another frequency. How they achieved this I don't know, but we certainly appreciated their strenuous efforts. We, on the other hand, only had to twist the 'channel' switch, and the tuning unit did the rest. The tuning unit also allowed us to place the radio where we wanted it, and to place the aerial tuning unit itself where the aerials came into the cabin.

We were in touch with the Australian Coastal Radio Stations until well away from Australian waters. The daily weather reports were then passed on through VJM Macquarie Island and VLZ Davis. The operators in the Antarctic station and Coastal Radio Stations cannot be thanked enough for their efforts in getting our sometimes faint messages through.

Although we could communicate with the Radphone operators in Sydney from Antarctic waters our signal was not considered of good enough quality for connecting to the telephone system. Actually, we found it hard to get a word in edgewise with *Queen Elizabeth II* and *Arcadia* passengers using the powerful ship's radios at short range to Sydney.

Pieter Arriens also took his own tranceiver, an Atlas 210X, and a manual aerial tuning unit. He was able to talk with Ham Radio operators in Australia most nights and communicate by morse code on other nights — mostly on the 10 metre bands. The Ham Radio equipment had the advantage of being able to move up or down in frequency when interference was observed. In poor atmospheric conditions Australian amateurs and the Antarctic Radio Operators spent hours with Pieter getting messages through. It is surprising how one or two personal messages can suddenly dispel the dreariness of long weeks of isolation.

The boat's batteries were 24 Volts positive earth. The radios required 12 Volts negative earth. This conflict was resolved by having separate batteries. A switch was used to isolate the radio battery from the charging system completely before connecting the battery to the radio. The charging system was simply a light bulb connected to the 24 Volt domestic batteries. The bulb limited the charging current to about 2 amps. The heat the bulb generated kept the Ham Radio and Aerial Matching Unit dry because they were in a specially-built cabinet with the bulb.

Radio interference from the generators could have been quite a problem, but *Solo* had switches fitted in the field circuit of the three generators so they could be 'silenced' during radio skeds.

Radar

I can highly recommend our Oak Seagle. Unfortunately the display console was placed near the cooking area. Even without the cooking, the roof was a mass of swaying drops of condensation. In a word, it was saturated. I believe the sweep transformer became saturated and its associated circuitry loaded down part of the power supply. Near Macquarie Island the fault was revealed when a power supply resistor overheated and unsoldered itself. I think a kinder climate, fewer pressure-cooker releasings nearby, and repeated operation to near overheating, dried the console out sufficiently for intermittent operation.

Satellite Buoy

The CSIRO lent us a cylindrical fibre-glass buoy about five feet long and one and a half feet in diameter. It was totally enclosed and self-contained. Solar cells charged its own batteries, and a transmitter in the fin transmitted daily to a NASA satellite. NASA could, along with many other such buoys, record our position once or twice a day to within about 1km. The CSIRO use the buoys to plot the movement of ocean currents.

The enclosed transmitter is about two feet long and only a few inches in diameter. I feel these devices would be ideal for a distress system. A suitable transmitter of only a few watts could have some switches so that the type of craft, type of emergency, number, and durability of survivors, or 'just testing' could be transmitted to a satellite. One satellite covers the world at least once a day. Surely the cost would be recouped in the first few years when the cost of search parties is considered.

Direction Finder

We were donated a Brookes and Gatehouse direction finder. We had hoped we could use it to find Macquarie Island if the weather was not suitable. Alas, the Island did not sport any kind of low frequency beacon, so our experiments with the direction finder were just out of plain desperation. The only suitable signal that might have worked was the island's portable radios on 4mHz. With all our stays, mast, and rigging making dozens of electrical loops this effort was doomed to failure. Nearing Sydney and Wollongong however, the instrument was in its own element with the appropriate Radio Direction Beacons on a few hundred kilohertz.

The design of this instrument is interesting, for it doubles as a radio on low, medium and short waves. It has been designed with marine conditions in mind, and the rod antenna sports a built-in compass.

Self-Steering

This system was an old Wood and Freeman — model 420. No doubt this system was originally designed for fishing boats. It had its own compass situated near the steering compass. When the compass card moved, a metal spike on it touched one of two wire whiskers, thereby passing an electric current. The current was amplified by transistors and relays until it could drive a hefty DC motor connected to the steering wheel.

For a few weeks this motor exacted a heavy toll on the batteries. We later realised the wheel was getting pretty hard to turn even for us. Greasing the steering system solved the problem of flat batteries, but now the autopilot was failing because of compass-near-the-pole problems. The compass had to be removed because of its proximity to the main steering compass. On the way home after Macquarie Island the self-steering system worked for days on end and I can see why lone sailors openly worship even the simplest of these machines.

Walkie-Talkies

Dick Smith donated four 5-watt Midland walkie-talkies. These worked well for ship-to-shore communication until they received a dunking in salt-water. (Plastic bags also keep water in.) Although they were cleaned that night we had some problems with two of them. On return home these sets were stripped down and cleaned more carefully. This was all that was needed for restoration to full range.

Any battery-operated equipment that gets a salt-water dunking should have the batteries removed IMMEDIATELY. Otherwise the battery voltage will assist corrosion by electrolysis and guarantee future unreliable operation.

Chronometer

Philips donated an Electronic clock — 'HF — QUARTZ ELECTRONIC'. Any navigator would find one of these a boon. They are not expensive, and their accuracy is excellent. The crystal frequency is close to 4mHz. Crystals of the appropriate type in this frequency range exhibit small variation due to temperature change. With care, the small trim capacitor beside the crystal can be tweaked for frequency correction, but this procedure can take months because a long time must elapse to see if the clock is too fast or too slow. There is no flywheel escapement for the boat's motion to influence. A solenoid indexes a ratchet one tooth each second.

Dry Cell Batteries

As temperatures drop to zero, carbon-zinc batteries are supposed to lose efficiency. Since Eveready donated quite an armload we decided to compensate by just using more of them. We used mainly the D cells in a variety of equipments and no short battery life was noticed.

Inverter

Flick a switch, listen for a little whine in the lazarette, and there it is: 240 Volts AC for a shaver or electric drill. With battery operated equipment nowadays this equipment would be considered superfluous. In Vic Meyer's day it was useful, so he installed it.

Apart from the landings I enjoyed most of all those long breezy days where we could all get together inside and have a meal or sing-song without worrying about watches or relieving whomever was on watch. The autopilot was in command. The sails drove us home at a cracking pace. The sailing generator charged the massive batteries at a useful 7 amps average — more than enough for the autopilot, lights, winches, and radios. Electrical systems, serviced as they deserve, work well and can save much labour and boredom. I feel that the decision to require someone with electrical knowledge to accompany the survey was a wise decision, and on the next trip south I hope to be there.

Appendix 5

The Ship Douglas Mawson and the Oceanic Research Foundation

by
David Lewis

A PIONEERING VESSEL

We have embarked on a far more ambitious project than we ever envisaged, even as lately as the completion of the main body of this book — no less than the designing and building of the ideal small ice ship.

Detailed investigations and calculations helped by leading naval architects have shown that it is possible to construct a strong and simple steel vessel in Australia. *Douglas Mawson* will, therefore, be built from scratch, designed by a team of Australian naval architects including Alan Payne. The ship will be immensely strong (of 20 mm steel, twice the thickness of a destroyer) and so shaped that ice pressure will lift her out of the ice instead of crushing her. This revolutionary principle was used in the famous *Fram* that drifted successfully past the North Pole. It is only applicable to relatively small ships and we propose to update it with modern materials and technology.

The 'squeeze-up' design will enable the little *Douglas Mawson* (about twenty-four metres long) to research ice-bound areas inaccessible to any but the largest icebreakers. She will be capable of twelve months' independent operation with a complement of ten, or five months with a complement of twenty, carrying scientific and expedition equipment in addition to fuel and stores.

The provisional lay-out of our ship is indicated above. The cost will be kept to a minimum by adopting extreme simplicity in equipment and accommodation for the volunteer crew and scientists. The straightforward and effective rig is a well-tried one that will be particularly well-suited for the long Southern Ocean passages, where the need for substantial expenditure of fuel will be obviated.

The cost of the ship will be around $200 000 and our newly-launched appeal for funds is already bearing fruit. We are offering in return public thanks and publicity but, infinitely more important, the opportunity to participate in a great pioneering venture. For *Douglas Mawson* will be the only research ship anywhere in the world to have such freedom to remain safely in the frozen seas. Some fields of research, eg krill's life cycle beneath

137

the winter pack-ice and measurements of this ice itself, will be open to her alone.

She will be unique.

'DOUGLAS MAWSON'

'FRAM' sections

1 Frames
2 Stanchions under deck-beams
3 Braces
4 Iron bars
5 Boiler
6 Main hold
7 Lower hold

0 1 2 3 4 5 6 7 8 9 10 Metres

THE OCEANIC RESEARCH FOUNDATION

Many opportunities exist for carrying out useful research in the less accessible parts of the world. Despite the large programs undertaken by governments and other bodies there are still many areas, geographic and scientific, awaiting investigation. These are more suited to small cost-effective expeditions.

The Foundation was set up in 1977 to study the fragile environments of Antarctica, Oceania and Australian coastal waters. Diminishing world resources and growing populations must inevitably bring more people to inaccessible places, but we still have the opportunity to foresee and forestall unnecessary damage that may result from ill-considered development projects and to help ensure that development is ecologically harmonious.

The Australian government has recognised and encouraged the Foundation which, while carrying out private expeditions, will continue to work in close consultation with government bodies and universities. The Foundation has been approved as a research institute for tax free donations under section 73A (6) of the Australian Income Tax Act. Its patron is Lord Shackleton and its technical adviser Sir Edmund Hillary; the expeditioners and scientists are unpaid.

Although Antarctica is the world's last great wilderness area and a matchless natural laboratory for which Australia and New Zealand have special responsibility due to their proximity, the Foundation's activities are far from being confined to it. A number of ventures are currently in train. For example, an on-going project to monitor the numbers of Fairy penguins on an island twenty-five kilometres north of Sydney is under way, thanks to the cooperation of National Parks and Wildlife. Again, in association with the Anthropology Department of Sydney University and the Australian Museum, the Foundation has initiated a study of the ancient 'naked eye' navigational techniques used aboard the sailing *proas* of Indonesia. The first reconnaissance will take place in 1979.

The Foundation appeals to readers, not only in Australia but throughout the world, to join us in researching and so safeguarding the last unspoilt frontiers of man's natural heritage.

David Lewis
Dangar Island
NSW 2253
tel 02 / 4551275
June 1979

ACKNOWLEDGMENTS

So many people and organisations contributed to the success of the expedition that we who took part are overwhelmed with gratitude — and a feeling of humility. It is almost inevitable that some may be unwittingly omitted. To any such I tender my sincere apologies and beg them to be tolerant of human error. To all I tender my profound thanks on behalf of the crew and the Oceanic Research Foundation.

Literary Acknowledgments

Miss Edgeworth David, for permission to quote the lines inscribed in the copy of *Home of the Blizzard* presented by Sir Douglas Mawson to her father. Mr Gareth M Thomas, Mawson's grandson, for the same. Information contained in Sparks and Soper's *Penguins* (Sydney: Angus and Robertson, 1968) has been invaluable in writing this book, as have historical and other background information made available by the Australian and New Zealand Antarctic Divisions.

Finally, without the diaries and other writings generously made available by other members of the expedition this account would have been woefully one-sided.

Official Support

We would like to thank the Minister for Science, Senator Webster, personally, for his unfailing encouragement of our enterprise and Dr Garrod, Director of the Antarctic Division, Department of Science, for allocating communications facilities and arranging scientific consultation and liaison. It is invidious to pick out individuals among so many but we are particularly indebted to Dr Bill Budd, Dr Knowles Kerry and Norman Linton-Smith. At the Bureau of Meteorology of the Department of Science, Mr HR Philpot was our liaison. We would like to thank him and his colleagues. The CSIRO Oceanography and Fisheries at Cronulla provided the 'Snow Petrel' satellite tracking device that was an invaluable adjunct to our scientific program. The director, Dr George Cresswell, and Mr Robin Austin were particularly helpful. Captain John Jepson US Navy, of the Fleet Weather Facility Suitland, kindly arranged for us to receive invaluable satellite ice reports.

140

Scientific Committee

We wish to thank the Foundation's Scientific Committee: Dr Embleton, Dr Frakes, Professor Lovering and Dr Recher, as well as Dr McCredie of the CSIRO for his helpful guidance.

Financial Support

Our enterprise would have been impossible without Dick Smith's generous donations, his organisational support and his guidance in financial matters.* He was unanimously elected the first Fellow of the Foundation. Grant Hawley, another donor and an original and continuing supporter, has become our second Fellow. Grateful thanks go to the Australian Broadcasting Commission, particularly to Mr Humphrey Fisher who purchased the television rights of the expedition; also to Mr Bob Connolly, producer of the film. Thanks are due to Mr Glenn Hamilton, Head of ABC Merchandising, who purchased the rights to this book. Other major financial contributors in alphabetical order were: Margaret Arriens, Bertie Barkell, Ron Barragry, Leslie Denham, Pat Earhart, Margaret Huenerbein, Dr Gavin and Kate Johnstone, Yvonne Liechti, Jutta and Sergei Malnic, Mountain Travel USA, Patricia Pedersen, Colin and Jane Putt, Dr and Mrs D Taylor, Brian Wall, Messrs Collier Watson NZ.

Gifts or loan of Equipment

Beaufort Distributors, Allied Polymer Group, provided our inflatable surfboat, the invaluable 'rubber duck' and also an emergency life raft. Outboard Marine Australia Pty Ltd provided the trusty 25 hp Evinrude that powered 'rubber duck' in extremely adverse conditions, as well as assorted petrol tanks and spares.

Maurice Findlay provided and fitted the excellent Stingray radio – his personal exertions in installing the set and obtaining the necessary crystals are described in the text.

Dick Smith provided the walkie-talkie radios upon which vital ship-to-shore communication depended, as well as numerous items of electronic equipment.

Paddy Pallin Ltd and Paddy Made Sales Pty Ltd through the exertions of Fritz Schaumberg, our equipment manager for *Solo* and Pallin's Canberra manager, and the cooperation of Paddy Pallin himself provided cold weather and alpine gear for the whole *Solo* party. Among the items were gloves and mitts, sleeping bags, waterproof clothing, Alliance Freeze-dried food, ice axes, alpine ropes, tents, et cetera.

Victor Rose of Marlins provided several of us with his incomparable heavy weather gear. Mr Ron Harding helped with wet suits and scuba gear. Mr Marks of Brandts Pty gave us our efficient kerosene stoves. Harvey Higgins of Mobil Oil provided our fuel, lubricants and kerosene. Mr Gannon of Dulux gave us our paint. John Evans made *Solo's* protective dodger free of charge. Philips Consumer Products presented us with a quartz crystal clock for our navigation and myself with a battery-powered electric razor. Equally welcome for navigation was the set of Antarctic maps presented by the New Zealand High Commission. Warburton Franki (Sydney) Pty Ltd lent us a radio direction finder. Mr B Harvey of AJ Chown

---

* He was even thoughtful enough to provide Yvonne a ticket for the Antarctic overflight.

Engineering loaned high pressure hull cleaning equipment. Mr Warner and Mr John-Paul Fauvarque of CIG Ltd supplied welding equipment. Both the ABC and *Seacraft* gave us film. Namco Houseware presented us with our two excellent pressure cookers. Kimberly-Clark Pty Ltd provided those essentials, toilet and kitchen paper, Union Carbide — Eveready Alkaline cell batteries. Last but not least Messrs D Roots and R Russell of Macquarie University constructed our bottom sampling winch and bucket.

Gifts of Food

Australian firms provided free of charge food, fuel and medical supplies for *Solo's* eight-man crew for our three months' expedition as well as a year's emergency food and fuel. At final count the Foundation itself had to spend less than $400 on sundries. It is very difficult to find words to express our gratitude to these many enterprising and generous firms. All contributed substantially to us. Where I have mentioned quantities of goods it is not to make invidious distinctions but to give the reader some idea of the stupendous quantities involved. Allowrie Products, 20 lbs butter and 24 kilos honey. George Andronicus, coffee and tea. Angus Park Fruit Co, 17 kilos dried fruits. Cadbury Schweppes, cocoa, marmalade and chocolate. Cerebos Aust Ltd, 36 kilos cereals and salt. CSR, exhibition materials, Fesq and Co, Gerald Buttrose and Bill Fesq, provided a most important staple in the form of three cases of Old Mill Rum. Ken Grubb, Canberra butcher, provided more than 50 lb of prime steak that lasted us nine days. Heinz and Co gave us many varieties of canned goods (nearly half a tonne). Kraft Foods Ltd provided cheese and Vegemite. Marrickville Holdings, peanut butter. Barry Marshall, dried bananas and Kendall mint cakes. Nabisco Pty Ltd, cracker biscuits (our bread substitute). Nestles Australia, a variety of their products totalling over 171 kilos soups and milk products. Plumrose Aust Ltd, assorted canned meats, et cetera (much of our staple diet). Rice Marketing Board, 20 kilos of rice. Rosella Foods Pty Ltd, dried vegetables (another staple), soups and jam. Solo, soft drinks. SPC Golden Valley Canners, some 32 kilos of canned fruit and vegetables. White Rose Flour Mills, 144 kilos flour. White Wings Ltd, 120 kilos of cereal and cake mix, et cetera. Unilever, 50 lb margarine and much help besides contributed by Peter Dunstan and Barbara Eddy (see under Services). Peter Doyle of Doyle Seafoods.

Medical Supples

Through the hard work of Murray Shanley MPS, who contacted all the firms named individually, a very complete medical kit was provided. It is noteworthy that not a single firm refused its full co-operation. Alcon Laboratories, Beiersdorf Ltd, Burroughs Welcome, Dista Products, Knoll Laboratories, May and Baker, Parke Davis, Roche Products, Rosken Laboratories (Fisons), ER Squibb and Sons.

Services

Captain Dodswell, the Sydney Harbourmaster, and the Marine Services Board, particularly in the persons of Captains Arthurson and Duffy and Mr Harvey and Mr Hughes allowed us to moor at Circular Quay in Sydney Cove, where they afforded us the most generous facilities, so contributing materially to the financing of the expedition. Captain Walker of the Public Transport Commission was no less helpful. Our stay at Circular Quay was enormously facilitated by Peter Dunstan and Barbara Eddy of Unilever, who gave us much-needed shower facilities as well as free use of their telephones. The Jack Wilson Motor Surf Rescue Group instructed us in the handling of 'Rubber Duck' in surf (I personally would have benefited from further instruction). We are most grateful to all the members, especially Mr Webster and Mr Matheson, for their patience. Sir Adrian Curlewis, patron of the club, was kind enough to launch us on our voyage. We also wish to thank Tim Curnow, the Foundation's literary agent who, as always, did far more than his professional part. We would like also to thank all those many ladies and gentlemen of the media who (even if sometimes badgered by Yvonne!) gave us such wonderful, fair-minded and accurate coverage.

Helpers

The task of acknowledging unselfish and vital help is no easier than that of adequately thanking our donors and sponsors; there were so many who played their parts in various ways. Jim and later John Marland spent months doing full-time unpaid work on *Solo*. So did Graham Cox just as he did years before on *Ice Bird*. Colin Putt assisted by his son Gerard directed the alterations and modifications and himself worked tirelessly. Norma Henderson sewed sails in her spare time. Ces Turner allowed us the facilities of his home on Dangar Island and did much of the welding. Louise Crossley made the lee boards that kept us in our bunks in bad weather. Many residents of Dangar Island and the vicinity became involved in ways varying from a fund-raising dinner to typing, among them Gwen Long, Sue and Richard Smith. Further afield, many activities were undertaken by Jane Putt, Dot Butler, Pat Findlay (typing), Stella Gottlieb and her stalwart friends, Stephen, Liz and Rosie Morrow, Peter and Wendy Parsons, Jutta Malnic, Wayne Sullivan and members of *Solo's* crew. The tireless co-ordinator and organiser of all this endeavour was Yvonne Liechti. Bertie Barkell, the Foundation's solicitor, was most helpful. Sheri Cowan and Barry Higgins were among our many cheerful helpers at Circular Quay. Not content with supplying our Stingray radio, Maurice Findlay worked *all night* on its installation on the eve of our departure.

Radio Communications

Special thanks are due to Pieter Arriens for organising our communications. The following Ham operators played a particularly important part: Barry White, our central contact of Sydney, Syd Molen of Sydney, Bill Hempell and Des Butler of Canberra; in the Antarctic Col Christiansen, and Harry Hocking aboard a Qantas Jumbo. Special thanks are due to the ANARE operators and those at McMurdo and to Meteo Melbourne and the personnel of the OTC coastal radio stations for their unfailing patience and courtesy.

Macquarie Island

Thanks would be grossly deficient if we omitted to pay tribute to the hospitality of Phil Pritchard and the whole of the ANARE contingent at Macquarie island.

Illustrations reproduced on pages 20 and 80, right, are from *A History of Polar Exploration* by David Mountfield (Hamlyn) (Radio Times Hulton Picture Library, London).

Illustration reproduced on page 80, left, is from *Antarctic Adventure* by Raymond E Priestley (Melbourne University Press).

Extract reproduced on page 41 is from *The Ascent of Rum Doodle* by W E Bowman (McDonald and Jane's).